The Spanish GCSE Handbook

A complete guide to getting a grade 9

About the author

Lucy Martin was educated in Brussels and the UK and has a First-Class degree in Modern Languages from Wadham College, Oxford. She speaks five languages and teaches to all levels, with a superb track record in top exam results. She is a contributor to BBC Bitesize and has written twelve books of her own for students of French, Spanish and German. She lives in London with her three children.

Third edition

Copyright Lucy Martin 2019

www.lucymartintuition.co.uk

Table of contents

Introduction

In my ten years of teaching Spanish, I have helped hundreds of students get top marks in their GCSEs. In this book I have put together everything you need to get through with flying colours.

The first section is a grammar revision chapter, and this is followed by a full set of oral answers with English translations using top phrases which will have your examiner ticking boxes like crazy. One size does not fit all, and you may pick and choose which phrases you include in your own work. Once those answers are in your head, you'll be able to use them not only in the oral exam but in the writing paper. My section on writing includes a simple mnemonic that will ensure you have all bases covered in the essay-writing section of the exam. By checking through your work using the mnemonic you can vastly increase your chances of success.

Part 4 covers the reading paper which is first and foremost a test of your understanding of written Spanish and includes a comprehension where you are required to answer in Spanish. This involves not only understanding the question and the text itself, but also finding the necessary information and putting it into the correct format.

The listening exam is the hardest. Without the chance to go back and hear things a third time, you need to adopt a strategy for "bulk" listening, whereby you take on board as much information as possible, without panicking over the odd word that you don't understand. There is no substitute for practice (and all exam boards provide past papers online) but there are plenty of top tips which will make the whole process more straightforward.

Best of luck with your revision and remember I am available to answer any questions through my website:

www.lucymartintuition.co.uk

PART 1

Grammar

Gender

Spanish nouns are masculine or feminine. Generally, the ones that end in a are feminine and the rest are masculine

El teatro	the theatre (masculine)
La biblioteca	the library (feminine)
Un cine	a cinema (masculine)
Una casa	a house (feminine)

but there are a few exceptions!

Nouns ending in -*ma* are masculine

el problema, el programa, el tema (theme), el dilema

Some nouns ending in a are masculine

el día, el mapa, el sofá, el planeta.

Words in -tion in English are -ción in Spanish and they are all feminine

reservación, conversación, contaminación, acción, atención, colaboración, clasificación, colección, combinación, concentración, condición, construcción, nación, operación, discriminación, publicación

Words in -ty in English are -dad and they are all feminine

universidad, sociedad, ciudad (city), calidad (quality), capacidad, comunidad, curiosidad, deformidad, dificultad, cantidad (quantity), velocidad, diversidad, creatividad, celebridad

Articles

Definite articles

There are 4 words for "the" in Spanish depending on whether the noun is masculine or feminine and singular or plural:

el perro	the dog
los perros	the dogs
la chica	the girl
las chicas	the girls
el chico	the boy
los chicos	the boys
la casa	the house
las casas	the houses

Indefinite articles

There are two words for "a" depending on whether the noun is masculine or feminine:

un gato	a cat
una mesa	a table
un chico	a boy
una chica	a girl

Add an "s" or "os" for "some"

unos coches	some cars
unas chicas	some girls

Present tense

Conjugating a verb means adapting it to the person who is doing it. In English, present tense conjugation is mostly straightforward. We keep the verb the same whoever is doing it, except that with the he/she/it form we add an s *(I eat, you eat, he/she eats, we eat, you eat, they eat)*.

We need to conjugate verbs in Spanish, but we don't need to include the pronoun. The ending of the verb tells you who is doing it. So, for example, if you see a *"mos"* on the end of a verb, the person who is doing it is going to be "we". *"Visitamos"* means *"we visit"*.

Although you don't have to use the pronouns (I, you, he, she, it, we, they), it is sometimes useful to know them for the purposes of your understanding, and for clarity or emphasis:

yo	I
tú	you (singular)
él	he
ella	she
usted	you (singular polite form)
nosotros	we
vosotros	you (plural)
ellos	they (masculine or mixed group)
ellas	they (feminine group)
ustedes	you (plural polite form)

You will notice a few things about this list. Firstly, there are two words for *"they"* depending on whether the group referred to is exclusively feminine or not. So, if you are talking about houses (casas), it would be *"ellas"*, otherwise *"ellos"*. Secondly, they have the polite "you" form that we don't have in English.

Regular verbs in the present (irregulars on next page)

-ar **hablar** (to speak)	-er **comer** (to eat)	-ir **vivir** (to live)
hablo	como	vivo
hablas	comes	vives
habla	come	vive
hablamos	comemos	vivimos
habláis	coméis	vivís
hablan	comen	viven
Similar verbs: ayudar – to help preparar – to prepare escuchar – to listen to bailar – to dance cantar – to sing limpiar – to clean trabajar – to work estudiar – to study visitar – to visit esperar – hope/ wait buscar – to look for mirar – to look at ganar – to earn, win comprar – to buy pagar – to pay (for) necesitar – to need pintar – to paint dibujar – to draw llegar – to arrive charlar – to chat cocinar – to cook contestar – to answer gastar – to spend	Similar verbs: aprender – to learn beber – to drink comprender – to understand deber – to have to esconder – to hide responder – to answer vender – to sell	Similar verbs: abolir – to abolish añadir – to add aplaudir – to applaud abrir – to open asistir a – to attend confundir – to confuse decidir – to decide definir – to define describir – to describe descubrir – to discover cubrir – to cover discutir – to discuss escribir – to write interrumpir – to interrupt prohibir – to prohibit recibir – to receive unir – to unite

Irregular verbs		
hacer – to do	**poner - to put**	**salir – to go out**
hago	pongo	salgo
haces	pones	sales
hace	pone	sale
hacemos	ponemos	salimos
hacéis	ponéis	salís
hacen	ponen	salen
tener – to have	**venir – to come**	**empezar – to begin**
tengo	vengo	empiezo
tienes	vienes	empiezas
tiene	viene	empieza
tenemos	venimos	empezamos
tenéis	venís	empezáis
tienen	vienen	empiezan
ser – to be	**estar – to be**	**ir – to go**
soy	estoy	voy
eres	estás	vas
es	está	va
somos	estamos	vamos
sois	estáis	vais
son	están	van
poder – to be able	**jugar – to play**	**volver – to return**
puedo	juego	vuelvo
puedes	juegas	vuelves
puede	juega	vuelve
podemos	jugamos	volvemos
podéis	jugáis	volvéis
pueden	juegan	vuelven
decir – to say	**dar – to give**	**pensar – to think**
digo	doy	pienso
dices	das	piensas
dice	da	piensa
decimos	damos	pensamos
decís	dais	pensáis
dicen	dan	piensan

The preterite (past) tense

Hablar (to speak)	Comer (to eat)	Vivir (to live)
hablé	comí	viví
hablaste	comiste	viviste
habló	comió	vivió
hablamos	comimos	vivimos
hablasteis	comisteis	vivisteis
hablaron	comieron	vivieron
hacer – to do	**poner - to put**	**poder – to be able**
hice	puse	pude
hiciste	pusiste	pudiste
hizo	puso	pudo
hicimos	pusimos	pudimos
hicistéis	pusistéis	pudisteis
hicieron	pusieron	pudieron
tener – to have	**venir – to come**	**dar – to give**
tuve	vine	di
tuviste	viniste	diste
tuvo	vino	dio
tuvimos	venimos	dimos
tuvisteis	venisteis	disteis
tuvieron	vinieron	dieron
Ser and ir –to be/go	**estar – to be**	**decir – to say**
fui	estuve	dije
fuiste	estuviste	dijiste
fue	estuvo	dijo
fuimos	estuvimos	dijimos
fuisteis	estuvisteis	dijisteis
fueron	estuvieron	dijeron

The perfect tense

The structure of the perfect tense, equivalent to the English "I have eaten" is made up of a person (*I*), an auxiliary ("have") and a past participle ("eaten"). The auxiliary ("have") is not the verb *tener*, but another verb (haber) used specifically to make this tense. The past participle is made by removing the ar/er/ir and adding -ado or -ido to the verb. You will see that -ar verbs go to -ado and that -er and -ir verbs both go the same way - *ido*.

Hablar (to speak)	**Comer** (to eat)	**Vivir** (to live)
He hablado	He comido	He vivido
Has hablado	Has comido	Has vivido
Ha hablado	Ha comido	Ha vivido
Hemos hablado	Hemos comido	Hemos vivido
Habéis hablado	Habéis comido	Habéis vivido
Han hablado	Han comido	Han vivido

Irregular past participles include:

hacer – hecho	ver – visto	volver - vuelto
decir – dicho	abrir – abierto	escribir – escrito
morir – muerto	poner – puesto	romper - roto

Using the preterite and the perfect tense

Use the preterite in Spanish when you'd use the *I ate* past tense in English, and the perfect tense when you'd say *I have eaten* in English.

The pluperfect tense (to say I *had* done something) is made using the infinitive, instead of the present of haber before the past participle: Había, habías, había, habíamos, habíais, habían

---

The near future tense

This is the easiest tense to use as it relies on conjugating only one verb – the verb ir – to go:

Voy a ir a España – I'm going to go to Spain

Vamos a comer pasta – We are going to eat pasta

ir = to go

voy	I go (or am going)
vas	you go
va	he / she / it goes
vamos	we go
vais	you (plural) go
van	they go

Examples of this future tense in action – don't forget the a

No vamos a salir	We are not going to go out
Van a trabajar	They are going to work
Vamos a comer tapas	We are going to eat tapas
Voy a visitar sitios turísticos	I'm going to visit tourist sights
Van a ir a la playa	They are going to go to the beach
Voy a dormir	I am going to sleep
¿Vas a jugar?	Are you going to play?
¿Vais a ir?	Are you (pl) going to go?
¿No vas a venir?	Aren't you going to come?
No voy a beber	I'm not going to drink
Vamos a ver…	We shall see…

The simple future tense

Hablar (to speak)	Comer (to eat)	Vivir (to live)
hablaré	comeré	viviré
hablarás	comerás	vivirás
hablará	comerá	vivirá
hablaremos	comeremos	viviremos
hablaréis	comeréis	viviréis
hablarán	comerán	vivirán

This tense must be used in your writing and speaking as well as the near future. Don't think too much about when to use which one. A general mish-mash of both will usually do. The thing is to watch out for the exceptions to the rule that the future root is the infinitive:

tener	**tendr**é	I will have
salir	**saldr**é	I will go out
hacer	**har**é	I will do / make
poner	**pondr**é	I will put
haber	**habr**á	there will be
decir	**dir**é	I will say
poder	**podr**é	I will be able to
venir	**vendr**é	I will come
querer	**querr**é	I will want
saber	**sabr**é	I will know

El fin de semana que viene, pondré la mesa y comeré con mis padres y también tendré que lavar el coche. *Next weekend I will lay the table, I will eat with my parents and I'll also have to wash the car.*

The conditional tense

Hablar (to speak)	Comer (to eat)	Vivir (to live)
hablaría	comería	viviría
hablarías	comerías	vivirías
hablaría	comería	viviría
hablaríamos	comeríamos	viviríamos
hablaríais	comeríais	viviríais
hablarían	comerían	vivirían

The endings go on the future root, which is usually the infinitive unless it's one of the irregulars on the list above. This tense is the "would" tense, so use it where you would say "would" in English.

Viviría en Londres	I would live in London
Comería muchas verduras	I would eat lots of vegetables
Haría más ejercicio	I would do more exercise

For the beginning of this type of sentence, you will need the past subjunctive. Don't worry too much about its formation, (the root is the third person plural of the preterite, for those who want to know) but the key phrases you need for GCSE are:

Si hubiera más rutas para ciclistas	If there were more cycle paths
Si pudiera cambiar algo	If I could change something
Si fuera alcalde / madre / rico	If I was mayor / a mother / rich
Si tuviera mucho dinero	If I had lots of money

Now add your conditional verb on the end, to form an *if* sentence.

The imperfect tense

This tense is used mainly to describe what used to happen in the past, rather than one-off events where you use the preterite or the perfect tense.

Hablar (to speak)	Comer (to eat)	Vivir (to live)
hablaba	comía	vivía
hablabas	comías	vivías
hablaba	comía	vivía
hablábamos	comíamos	vivíamos
hablabais	comíais	vivíais
hablaban	comían	vivían

There are only three exceptions:

Ser – era (I used to be)

Ir – iba (I used to go)

Ver – veía (I used to watch / see)

Here is a passage that shows the use of the three past tenses, the perfect, preterite and imperfect

He visitado muchos paises. Cuando era pequeña, iba a España cada año. Me gustaba mucho porque había mucho que hacer y hacía sol todo el tiempo. Pero el año pasado fuimos a Francia. No me gustó nada porque no podía hablar español.

I have visited many countries. When I was little we went to Spain every year. I liked it because there was lots to do and it was sunny all the time. But last year we went to France. I didn't like it at all because I wasn't able to speak Spanish.

The present subjunctive

This is another bonus tense, as in it isn't strictly essential but will catapult you into a new grade bracket if you can shoehorn it in to your writing and speaking.

It is used after *que* in expressions relating to importance, purpose, negative thinking, emotion and wanting someone to do something.

How to form the subjunctive

To form it, the general rule is that you take the first person singular (the I or yo form) of the present tense, remove the final o and add either an e (if it's an -ar verb like hablar) or an a (if it's an -er or -ir verb). I call this vowel swapping. It's as if the verbs are disguising themselves.

hablo goes to hable

como goes to coma

vivo goes to viva

The rest of the verb follows as you'd expect:

Hablar (to speak)	**Comer** (to eat)	**Vivir** (to live)
hable	coma	viva
hables	comas	vivas
hable	coma	viva
hablemos	comamos	vivamos
habléis	comáis	viváis
hablen	coman	vivan

There are 6 irregular subjunctives

dar (to give) - dé

estar (to be) - esté

ser (to be) - sea

ir (to go) - vaya

saber (to know)– sepa

haber (the auxiliary verb that forms the perfect tense) - haya

Use with expressions relating to importance

Es importante que reciclemos – It's important that we recycle.

Use with expressions relating to purpose

Para que mis amigos puedan venir – So that my friends can come

Use with expressions relating to negative thinking

No pienso que sea una buena idea – I don't think it's a good idea

Use with expressions relating to emotion

Estoy contenta de que seas aquí – I am happy you're here

Use with expressions about wanting someone to do something

Quiere que haga mis deberes – S/he wants me to do my homework.

Use with cuando in the future

Cuando sea mayor, seré profe – When I'm older I'll be a teacher.

Use with aunque (although)

Como mucho chocolate, aunque sea malo para la salud – I eat lots of chocolate, although it's bad for your health.

Adjectives

Adjectives usually go after the noun and will agree with it in gender and number. This means that if it ends in an *o*, this changes to an *a* if the noun it describes is feminine. If it ends in *-or* this changes to *-ora*, and they all get an extra *s* on the end (*-es* in the case of the ones ending in *-or*) if the noun they describe is plural. Adjectives ending in *e* like *inteligente* can't change to *a*, so they only agree in number.

Vivimos en casas interesantes	We live in interesting houses
Reciclo muchas botellas	I recycle a lot of bottles
Las pizzas son deliciosas	(The) pizzas are delicious
Hablo con personas inteligentes	I talk to clever people

Possessive adjectives

These go in front of and agree in number with the noun they refer to. So, the word for *my* when we say *my sister* (mi hermana) is different from when we say *my brothers* (mis hermanos). Here they all are:

mi hermano / hermana	my brother / sister
mis padres	my parents
tu hermano / hermana	your brothers / sisters
tus padres	your parents
su hermano / hermana	his, her or their brother / sister
sus padres	his, her or their parents
nuestro(s) hermano(s)	our brother(s)
nuestra(s) hermana(s)	our sister(s)
vuestro(s) hermano(s)	your (from you *pl*) brother(s)
vuestra(s) hermana(s)	your (from you *pl*) sister(s)

Test Repeat until you can put all the sentences into Spanish.

1.	They live in the house	Viven en la casa
2.	We live in a big house	Vivimos en una casa grande
3.	They live in his house	Viven en su casa
4.	The girls eat their fruit	Las chicas comen su fruta
5.	He lives in his apartment	Vive en su apartamento
6.	We eat lots of pizza	Comemos mucha pizza
7.	I have two big cars	Tengo dos coches grandes
8.	I don't have sisters	No tengo hermanas
9.	He speaks to my parents	Habla con mis padres
10.	We are speaking to my teacher	Hablamos con mi profesor
11.	There are some dogs in the park	Hay unos perros en el parque
12.	We don't speak Spanish	No hablamos español
13.	They don't speak English	No hablan inglés
14.	My parents live in Spain	Mis padres viven en España
15.	My children live in London	Mis amigos viven en Londres
16.	His brother doesn't eat pasta	Su amigo no come pasta
17.	There are good beaches in Spain	Hay playas buenas en España
18.	The teachers are good	Los profesores son buenos
19.	My parents are strict	Mis padres son estrictos
20.	There are two beers here	Hay dos cervezas aquí

Using infinitives

Spanish verbs are hard to conjugate. To avoid conjugating them, use one of these expressions followed by an infinitive:

1. **To say what you like and don't like – me gusta**

No me gusta trabajar	I don't like working
Me gusta dormir	I like sleeping

2. **To say what you usually do - suelo**

Suelo comer mucha fruta	I usually eat a lot of fruit
No suelo llegar tarde	I don't usually arrive late

3. **To say what you have to or can do – tengo que**

Tengo que salir	I have to go out
Tenemos que trabajar	We have to work
No tengo que ir	I don't have to go
No tenemos que escuchar	We don't have to listen

4. **To say what you can do – puedo**

¿Puedo venir?	Can I come?
¿Pueden salir?	Can they go out?
No puedo hacer mucho	I can't do much

5. **To say what you want to do – quiero**

Quiero comprar un bocadillo	I want to buy a sandwich
Quieren ir al cine	They want to go to the cinema

6. **To make the FUTURE TENSE – voy a**

Voy a vivir en España	I am going to live in Spain
No voy a comer mucho	I am not going to eat much

Adding to infinitives

Here are some useful additions to those infinitives

Jugar al futbol / tenis / golf – to play football

Rule of thumb is that when you play something – use *al* before the sport or game, and they are mostly the same word as English (cricket, hockey, rugby) but with a more phonetic spelling – *voleibol, tenis, netbol*.

Hacer deporte – to do sport

We don't "play" sport, we do it. It's the same with all the non-ball sports, you *hacer* most of them – *jogging, ciclismo, vela, patinaje* (jogging, cycling, sailing, skating).

Ver la tele – to watch TV

Remember to say *la* tele because in English we just "watch TV".

Ir al colegio en coche – to go to school by car

Al, which literally means "to the" is a combination of *a* and *el*. Sometimes it's logical (*"al* cine" means "*to the* cinema") but we have to remember that we go "to *the* school", not just to school.

Ir al colegio a pie – to go to school on foot

Whereas *by car* is *en coche*, if you are not taking transport, use *a*.

Ir de compras – to go shopping

Preparar la comida / cena – to cook lunch / dinner

They tend to prepare rather than make or cook food.

Hablar con mis amigos – to talk to my friends

You talk with people, not to them.

Escuchar música - to listen to music (the "to" is built in)

Ser and estar

You use *ser* **to describe the characteristics** of a thing or person, and *estar* **to describe states of emotion and position**. Most of the time, estar will be used with temporary states, to describe feelings / emotions and where someone or something currently is.

Here are the verbs conjugated in full:

ser (characteristic)	estar (emotion / position)	
soy	estoy	I am
eres	estás	you (s) are
es	está	he, she, it is
somos	estamos	we are
sois	estáis	you are
son	están	they are

Here are some examples of their use:

¿Dónde está el hotel?	Where is the hotel?
¿Tu hermano es simpático?	Is your brother nice?
La casa es muy grande (chara.)	The house is very big
La casa está en Londres (position)	The house is in London
La casa está sucia (currently)	The house is dirty
La cocina está limpia (currently)	The kitchen is clean
El hombre es timido (chara.)	The man is shy
El hombre está casado ('emotion')	The man is married
Los gatos están contentos (emotion)	The cats are happy
Somos importantes (chara.)	We are important

Adjectives that go with ser

grande	big
pequeño	small
alto	tall
bajo	short
nuevo	new
antiguo / histórico / viejo	old
guapo	good-looking
joven	young
turístico	touristy
animado	lively
tímido	shy
divertido	fun
aburrido	boring
interesante	interesting
importante	important
inteligente	intelligent
bueno	good
malo	bad
gordo	fat
delgado	thin
español / inglés	Spanish / English

Adjectives that go with estar

casado	married
separado	separated
divorciado	divorced
contento	happy
enfadado	angry
cansado	tired
furioso	furious
estresado	stressed

Positions with estar

en casa	at home
en Londres / España	In London / Spain
cerca de	near
lejos de	far from
delante de	in front of
detrás de	behind
al lado de	next to
debajo de	under

An extra use of estar – to say what you *are doing*

Spanish allows you to say that you are *in the process of* doing something as well as that you do it. You can say *I'm eating*, as well as *I eat*. This is what we call the present continuous.

Estoy hablando	I am talking
Estás escuchando	you are listening
Está jugando	s/he is playing
Estoy buscando	I'm looking for
Estamos trabajando	we are working
Estáis limpiando	you are cleaning
Están comiendo	they are eating
Estoy bebiendo	I am drinking
Estoy aprendiendo	I am learning
Están viendo la tele	they are watching TV
Estoy limpiando	I am cleaning
Estamos reciclando	we are recycling
Estamos comunicando	we are communicating
Estáis preparando	you (pl) are preparing
Está nadando	s/he is swimming
Está cantando	s/he is singing
Estamos esperando	we are waiting

Liking things

Expressing liking, using the verb *gustar*

Revise this by testing yourself on the examples below:

Me gusta bail**ar**	I like dancing
No me gusta nada limpi**ar**	I don't like cleaning at all
Me gusta el perro	I like the dog
Me gusta**n los perros**	I like dog**s**
No me gusta**n** nada **las manzanas**	I don't like apple**s** at all
Le gusta comer	S/he likes eating
Les gusta bailar	They like dancing
No les gusta**n los** mariscos	They don't like seafood
A mi hermano le gusta beber	My brother likes drinking
A mis padres les gustar comer	My parents like eating
A mi hermana no le gusta el sol	My sister doesn't like the sun
A Fernando no le gusta**n los** gatos	Fernando doesn't like cats

What do you observe here?

- Firstly, the structure is *"to me pleases X"* rather than *"I like X"*.

- Secondly, there is no -ing after the like verb. Use an infinitive instead.

- Thirdly, when the thing that you like is plural, you add an *n* to the liking verb. Where there's an *s* there's an *n*...

- To add a complication, if someone else likes something, we have to change the pronoun *me* to te, le, nos, os, or les.

Me gusta(n) *add n if the thing you like is plural*	I like
Te gusta(n)	you (s) like
Le gusta(n)	he/she likes
Nos gusta(n)	we like
Os gusta(n)	you (pl) like
Les gusta(n)	they like

- If we are naming the person who likes the thing, then add A just before their name.

A Fred le gusta bailar	Fred likes dancing
A Doris le gusta el chocolate	Doris likes chocolate
A mi hermana le gustan los gatos	My sister likes cats
A mis amigas les gusta el perro	My friends like the dog
A mis hermanos les gusta comer	My brothers like eating
A mis amigos les gustan los caramelos	My friends like sweets

The strange thing about gustar

The crucial point to note is that *the thing you like is the subject of the sentence.* That's why the verb *gustar* changes if the thing you like is plural. The thing you like *governs* the verb gustar; and that is also why you need to include the article el / la / los / las before the noun in each case. In English you can say "I like chocolate", in Spanish you need to say "me pleases the chocolate".

Pronouns

Using pronouns as direct objects (*eg. I see him / she sees me*)

Look at the verb ver = to see

veo	I see
ves	you (s) see
ve	he / she / it sees
vemos	we see
veis	you (pl) see
ven	they see

We can put personal pronouns in front of verbs (where in English they come after the verb)

he sees me	me ve (the "me" comes first)
you (s) see me	me ves
they see me	me ven

And it's not just me, it's you! (or him, her, it, us, them…)

lo veo	I see him (or it, with a masculine noun)
la veo	I see her (or it, with a feminine noun)
los veo	I see them (masculine)
las veo	I see them (feminine)
nos ven	they see us
nos ve	he / she sees us

More examples of pronouns

Lo vemos	We see him (or it, with a masculine noun)
La vemos	We see her (or it, with a feminine noun)
Los vemos	We see them (masculine)
Las vemos	We see them (feminine)
La como	I eat it (eg. la pizza)
Los como	I eat them (eg. los caramelos)
Las como	I eat them (eg. las fresas)
La bebo	I drink it (eg. la cerveza)
Las conozco	I know them (eg. las chicas)
Lo he comido	I have eaten it
Las he visto	I have seen them

Pronouns on the end of verbs

After an infinitive, or a gerund (which is the -ando -iendo ending), you can actually stick the pronoun on the end.

No me gusta verlo	I don't like seeing him / it
Quiero comerlos	I want to eat them
Suelen ayudarnos	They usually help us
Voy a beberla	I'm going to drink it (feminine)
Van a comprarlas	They are going to buy them
Va a ayudarme	He / she is going to help me.
Estoy comiéndolo	I'm eating it

Reflexive verbs

These exist to express things that you do to *yourself* ie. shower, wash, brush teeth, wake up and get up. You can shower (duchar) someone else, or you can shower yourself (duchar**se**). You can wash something or someone else (lavar) or wash yourself (lavar**se**). You can lift up something (levantar) or get yourself up out of bed (levantar**se**). If you want to use these verbs in the *I* form, in any tense just put *me* on the front (pronounced *"meh"* not *"me"*).

Me levanto	from levantarse	I get up
Me ducho	from ducharse	I shower
Me lavo	from lavarse	I wash (myself)
Me acuesto	from acostarse	I go to bed
Me visto	from vestirse	I get dressed
Me divierto	from divertirse	I have fun
Me quedo	from quedarse	I stay
Me relajo	from relajarse	I relax

Here's how it goes when it's other people doing it:

Me levanto	I get up
Te levantas	you get up
Se levanta	he / she gets up
Nos levantamos	we get up
Os levantáis	you (pl) get up
Se levantan	they get up

The personal *a*

If I say, "I see the boy", *the boy* is the direct object of the verb *to see*. Similarly, with "I help my friend", the *friend* is the direct object of the verb *to help*.

In Spanish, where the direct object of a verb is animate (ie. alive) then it must be preceded by the word "*a*", which normally means "*to*" but in this case is just recognition of the next noun being a living thing. You might imagine this to be putting some polite distance between you and the other person but bear in mind that it might be an animal too. If it is a masculine singular noun, you will need to condense the "*a*" and the "*el*" to form "*al*", so you can't say *veo a el perro*, you say *veo al perro*.

Here are some verbs you might use with an animate object and need the a:

ayudar	to help
mirar	to look at
pasear	to walk (eg. dog)
odiar	to hate
animar	to encourage
escuchar	to listen to
acompañar	to accompany
conocer	to know (a person)
buscar	to look for

Don't use the personal a with tener (*tengo un hermano* NOT *a un hermano*) or with non-specific things (*busco un marido* NOT *a un marido*)

PART 2

Speaking

The speaking exam is the one where you can get a long way through rote learning of prepared speeches and answers, but beware... You will also need to understand the questions, and with most exam boards take part in a role play where you will need to respond to instructions and ask your own questions.

Discussion - understanding questions

The first skill to master in your preparation for the oral exam is understanding the questions you are asked. The same question can be asked in a number of different ways. For example:

¿Cuáles son tus pasatiempos favoritos?

What are your favourite hobbies?)

¿Qué quieres hacer durante tu tiempo libre?

What do you like to do in your free time?)

¿Qué sueles hacer para divertirte?

What do you usually do to have fun?)

Test yourself on the structures below to make sure you are ready for all forms of question before practising your answers.

¿Cuáles son?	Which are / what are…?
¿Cuál es?	which is / what is…?
¿Qué?	what
¿A qué hora?	when (at what time?)
¿Cuando?	when (generally)?
¿Cómo?	how / what's it like?
¿Dónde?	where?
¿Quién?	who?
¿Por qué?	why?

Your presentation

Depending on your exam board, you may have to either describe a photo you have found yourself, answer questions on a photocard with a few minutes preparation time or make a speech lasting about a minute on one of the set topics.

Prepared speech (Cambridge IGCSE) and prepared photo (Edexcel IGCSE)

In the case of prepared speeches, make sure you maximize your use of impressive phrases, use all the tenses you can cram in, and leave the examiner to ask boring questions like "what is he / she wearing?"

Here is an example of a description of a picture: this happens to be a cartoon picture of a family on a beach holiday, with a sinister shark fin poking out of the water. This would be an Edexcel IGCSE full marks answer:

Esta foto fue tomada el año pasado cuando estábamos de vacaciones en Australia. Puedes verme a la izquierda, acostada en una toalla verde, mientras que mi prima está construyendo un castillo de arena. Cerca de mí, mi padre acaba de sacar una foto de mi hermano que está surfeando. Él es más valiente que yo y mi madre parece orgullosa de él porque esta lo mira sonriendo. ¡Pero quiere que sea cuidadoso! Lamentablemente, nadie ha notado la aleta del tiburón que está a punto de devorar a la mitad de mi familia. ¡Qué pesadilla! En el fondo, un joven está navegando en paracaídas, y él, como el piloto de la avioneta, hubiera tenido una vista magnífica del ataque de los tiburones. Todos tuvimos suerte ya que resultó que el tiburón no tenía hambre. Aparte de eso, fueron unas vacaciones perfectas y tengo ganas de volver allí cuando sea mayor.

Translation

This photo was taken last year when we were on holiday in Australia. You can see me on the left, lying on a green towel, while my cousin is building a sandcastle. Near me, my father has just taken a photo of my brother who is surfing. He is braver than me and my mother seems proud of him as she is looking at him with a smile. But she wants him to be careful! Unfortunately, nobody has noticed the fin of the shark which is about to devour half my family. What a nightmare! In the background, a young man is parasailing, and he, like the pilot of the small plane, would have had a magnificent view of the shark attack. We were all lucky as it turned out the shark wasn't hungry. Apart from that, this was a perfect holiday in a little corner of paradise and I can't wait to go back there when I'm older.

Follow up questions

After talking about a photo, you can expect a specific question relating to a particular person in it: **¿Qué hace?** Next, they may ask you about the weather: **¿Qué tiempo hace?** and some specific questions about various people in the picture, what they are wearing, doing, or saying.

Questions inviting the past tense

Next they will ask what happened before the photo **¿Qué pasó antes de la foto / más temprano ?** Be prepared to describe what happened before the photo – taking each person in turn, so you need to know your past tense verbs in the *he* and the *they* form:

Sample answer – Me desperté, me levanté y me vestí. Fui al restaurante donde y desayuné tostadas y fruta antes de ir a la playa. Hacía sol y tenía ganas de broncearme.

I woke up, got up and got dressed. I went to the restaurant where I had toast and fruit for breakfast before going to the beach. It was sunny and I wanted to sunbathe.

Alternative answers relating to other people in the picture in the he/they forms:

Se despertó / se despertaron	he/she or they woke up
Se levantó / se levantaron	he/she or they got up
Se vistió / se vistieron	he/she/they got dressed
Desayunó / desayunaron	he/she/they had breakfast
Tenía / tenían ganas de broncearse	he/she/they wanted to sunbathe

Questions inviting the future tense

Next they will ask what will happen after the photo. **¿Que pasará después de la foto?** Here you will need your future tense verbs as they relate to you and the others in the picture.

Sample answer – Después de pasar todo el día bronceándome voy a volver al hotel para ducharme antes de echarme una siesta. Al despertarme iré al restaurante para cenar.

After having spent the day sunbathing, I will go back to the hotel to take a shower before having a nap. When I wake up I will go to the restaurant to have dinner.

Alternative answers relating to other people in the picture in the he/they forms:

Va *or* van a volver

Para duchar**se**

Antes de echar**se**

Al despertar**se**

Irá *or* irán

Questions inviting the conditional

You are also likely to be asked a question inviting the conditional tense. ¿Como serian tus vacaciones ideales? This will involve the word *si (if)* followed by the imperfect subjunctive, then the conditional.

Sample answer - Si fuera rica iría a Francia. Tengo ganas de ir el año que viene con mi mejor amiga durante unas semanas. Nos alojaríamos en un hotel de cinco estrellas cerca de la playa. Pasaríamos todos los días relajándonos, jugando al tenis, nadando en el mar y tomando el sol. Haríamos nuevos amigos, probaríamos los platos típicos de la región y compraríamos recuerdos. Haría sol todos los días. ¡Qué perfecto!

If I was rich I would go to France. I would like to go next year with my best friend for a few weeks. We would stay in a five-star hotel near the beach. We would spend every day relaxing, playing tennis, swimming in the sea and sunbathing. We would make new friends, we would try the local dishes and buy souvenirs. It would be sunny every day. How perfect!

Clothes and accessories

Make sure you know the words for all the clothes items and accessories in the picture, and practise them with the colours, making sure to agree the colour with the gender and number of the item eg.

Lleva una camiseta blanc**a**	he's wearing a white Tshirt
Lleva zapatos neg**ros**	he's wearing black shoes
Llevan chaquetas amarill**as**	they are wearing yellow jackets
Llevan pantalones cort**os**	they are wearing shorts

Here's a reminder of the clothes and accessories vocabulary

una camisa — a shirt *(camisole)*

una camiseta — a Tshirt *(little camisa)*

pantalones — trousers *(pants are long)*

vaqueros — jeans

un vestido — a dress *(long vest)*

una falda — a skirt *(folded pleats?)*

los guantes — gloves

calcetines — socks *(concertina down legs)*

un cinturón — a belt *(from cintura=waist)*

una corbata — tie *(bat things away with it)*

una chaqueta — a jacket

gafas — glasses

un paraguas — umbrella *(para agua = for water)*

un jersey — a jumper

zapatos — shoes

zapatillas de deporte — trainers

un abrigo — an overcoat

un impermeable — a raincoat *(impermeable)*

un monedero — wallet *(your money der)*

una maleta — suitcase *(need a mallet to shut it)*

una bolsa — a bag

un reloj — a watch or clock

Top tips for the conversation

- **The examiner wants you to succeed** – so don't imagine that they are trying to trip you up. It is likely to be your own teacher testing you and he or she will want you to get the best result possible.

- **Listen for key words** such as

  ideal (inviting the conditional)

  joven (when you were younger, so imperfect)

  el fin de semana pasado (inviting preterite)

  el fin de semana que viene (inviting future)

  cambiar (what you'd like to change, so begin by saying what you don't like)

  prefieres (you will need to compare two things)

- **They are looking to tick boxes.** The recording will be sent off to moderators and needs to show your mastery of all the main tenses and a good knowledge of the language overall. So, if you keep getting asked the same type of question, then chances are you have not yet successfully demonstrated your knowledge of a particular tense.

- **Keep talking!** Stay on topic, but the more you speak the fewer questions will be asked, and the longer you are in control.

- **Take your time** before answering and remember you can ask the examiner to repeat a question.

- **Don't panic**. It will be over in a few minutes. Smile, breathe and enjoy!

HOUSE, HOME AND DAILY ROUTINE

Your house

Tengo suerte porque es la mejor casa del mundo y vivo allí desde hace cinco años. Mi casa es grande, moderna y cómoda. En la planta baja hay la cocina, el salón, el despacho y el comedor. En el primer piso hay cuatro dormitorios y un cuarto de baño. Detrás de la casa hay un gran jardín donde se puede jugar al futbol cuando hace buen tiempo. Lo que más me gusta es que ya no tengo que compartir mi dormitorio con mi hermano porque es tan molesto. Lo que no me gusta es el ruido del tráfico.

I am lucky because it is the best house in the world and I have been living there for 5 years. My house is big, modern and comfortable. On the ground floor there is the kitchen, the lounge, the office and the dining room. On the first floor there are four bedrooms and a bathroom. Behind the house is a big garden where you can play football when it is good weather. What I like most is that I no longer have to share my bedroom with my brother because he is so annoying. What I don't like is the traffic noise.

Your bedroom

Mi dormitorio está en el primer piso al lado del dormitorio de mis padres. Al lado de la cama hay un armario y delante de la ventana hay un escritorio donde hago mis deberes. Las paredes son azules porque es mi color favorito, y tengo suerte porque tengo no solo un ordenador portátil sino también una televisión, así que puedo fácilmente pasar muchísimas horas relajándome sin tener que bajar la escalera.

My bedroom is on the first floor by my parents' bedroom. Next to the bed there is a cupboard and in front of the window is a desk where I do my homework. The walls are blue because it's my favourite colour and I'm lucky because I not only have a laptop but also a television so I can easily spend many hours relaxing without having to go downstairs.

Ideal house

Si fuera rico me compraría mi casa ideal. Mi casa ideal sería enorme, moderna y cómoda, con una gran piscina para que pudiera hacer natación todos los días. Si fuera riquísima, habría también un cine donde pasaría muchísimas horas viendo películas con mis amigos, y un jardín con árboles y flores. Estaría cerca del centro de Londres para que mis amigos pudieran visitarme.

If I were rich, I would buy my ideal house. My ideal house would be enormous, modern and comfortable with a big pool so I could swim every day. If I was really rich there would also be a cinema where I would spend many hours watching films with my friends, and a garden with trees and flowers. It would be near the centre of London so that my friends could visit me.

Ideal family

No creo que haya la familia ideal. Lo importante es que el niño necesita el amor y la estabilidad, y el tipo de familia no importa. Lo importante es que puedas contar con tu familia. Hoy en día hay un montón de tipos de familia – con parejas homosexuales, familias monoparentales y tradicionales, familias numerosas, hijos únicos, y todos tienen su valor. Tengo suerte porque en mi familia nos llevamos bien.

I don't think there is such a thing as the ideal family – the important thing is that a child needs love and stability and the type of family doesn't matter. The important thing is to be able to rely on your family. Nowadays there are loads of different types of family – with homosexual couples, single parents, traditional families, large families and only children, and all have their value. I am lucky because in my family we get on well.

About you

Me llamo .... y tengo ..... años. Soy bastante grande, tengo los ojos azules y el pelo rubio. Soy muy divertido, deportista e inteligente, pero a veces un poco perezoso, sobre todo por la mañana cuando no tengo ganas de ir al colegio y tengo que pegarme un madrugón.

My name is .... and I'm ..... years old. I am quite tall, I have blonde hair and blue eyes. I am very funny, sporty, and intelligent but sometimes a bit lazy, especially in the mornings when I don't want to go to school and I have to get up early.

About your interests and hobbies

Cuando tengo tiempo / una vez a la semana / todos los días / el sábado, me gusta hacer ciclismo con mi padre y los fines de semana suelo jugar al tenis con mi amigo en el parque porque es mi deporte favorito y soy adicto. Tengo suerte porque soy miembro de un club de tenis desde hace dos años. Paso mucho tiempo viendo la televisión, aunque sea malo para la salud, para relajarme y olvidar el estrés del colegio. Tengo ganas de aprender el ajedrez porque me parece más interesante que ver la tele.

When I have time / once a week / every day / on Saturdays, I like to go cycling with my father and at the weekends I usually play tennis with my friend in the park because it's my favourite sport and I'm addicted to it. I'm lucky because I have been a member of a tennis club for 2 years. I spend a lot of time watching TV, although it is bad for your health, in order to relax and to forget the stress of school. I'd like to learn chess because it seems more interesting than watching TV.

Your family

En mi familia hay cinco personas, mi madre, mi padre, mis dos hermanos y yo. Mi hermano mayor es grande, delgado, muy guapo y más deportista que yo. Tiene el pelo marrón y los ojos verdes. Le gusta jugar al futbol y hacer la natación. Mi hermano menor tiene el pelo rubio y los ojos azules. Siempre hace el tonto. Nos parecemos mucho y nos llevamos bien pero cuando tiene un humor de perros, es harina de otro costal. Me llevo bastante bien con mis padres, pero a veces discutimos, porque no les gusta cuando vuelvo tarde a casa.

In my family there are 5 people: my mother, my father, my two brothers and me. My older brother is tall, slim, very handsome and sportier than me. He has brown hair and green eyes and likes football and swimming. My younger brother has blond hair and blue eyes. He is always messing about. We look very similar and we get on well, but when he's in a bad mood that's another matter entirely. I get on quite well with my parents, but sometimes we argue because they don't like it when I come home late.

Is marriage important?

No importa si estás casado o no, sobre todo porque tantos matrimonios fracasan, y el número de personas solteras crece. Muchos niños son testigos de divorcio y viven con hermanastros y hermanastras. No sé si voy a casarme o no. Me gustaría vivir con alguien durante unos años antes de tomar una decisión tan importante. Deberíamos aprender más sobre las relaciones en el colegio para que sepamos lo que supone el matrimonio.

It doesn't matter if you are married or not, especially because so many marriages break down and the number of single people is increasing. Lots of children have witnessed divorce and live with step=brothers and step-sisters. I don't know if I will get married or not. I'd like to live with someone for a few years before making such an important decision. We should learn more about relationships at school so that we know what marriage involves.

Describe your best friend

Tengo suerte porque tengo el mejor amigo del mundo que se llama …… Somos amigos desde hace diez años. Tiene los ojos azules y el pelo rubio. Es más grande que yo, pero menos deportista. Nos llevamos bien porque tenemos muchos pasatiempos en común – nos gustan los videojuegos y solemos ir de compras juntos todos los fines de semana. Además, tenemos lo mismo sentido de humor. ¡Qué suerte! Lo único es que no le gusta el futbol y yo soy fanático del Manchester United. Si le gustara el futbol sería perfecto.

I am lucky because I have the best friend in the world called ………… We have been friends for ten years. He has blue eyes and blonde hair. He is taller than me, but less sporty. We get on well because we have lots of hobbies in common – we like videogames and we usually go shopping together at the weekend. Also we have the same sense of humour. How lucky! The only thing is that he doesn't like football and I'm a Man United fan. If he liked football he would be perfect.

Recent outing with best friend

El fin de semana pasado fui con ……………… a Londres para ir de compras. Tuve que comprar un regalo para mi madre para su cumpleaños. Al llegar al centro, compramos muchísima ropa, y después comimos en una pizzería. ¡Qué deliciosa! Lo malo fue que casi olvidé de comprar un regalo para mi madre. Por suerte hay una tienda cerca de mi casa donde se venden libros interesantes sobre la naturaleza. Escogí un libro, lo compré y volví a casa. A mi madre le gustó muchísimo.

Last weekend I went with …………… to London to go shopping. I had to buy a present for my mother for her birthday. On arriving in the centre, we bought a lot of clothes and afterwards we ate lunch in a pizzeria. How delicious! The bad thing was that I almost forgot to buy a present for my mother. Luckily there is a shop near my house where they sell interesting books on nature. I chose a book, bought it and went home. My mother really loved it.

Future outing with best friend

El fin de semana que viene, vamos a ir de compras para buscar nueva ropa. Después iremos al cine para ver la nueva película de James Bond porque nos encantan las películas de acción. Antes de volver a casa cenaremos en un restaurante con nos compañeros de clase y discutiremos la película.

Next weekend we are going to go shopping to look for new clothes. Afterwards we will go to the cinema to see the new Bond film because we love action films. Before going home, we will have dinner in a restaurant with our school friends and we will discuss the film.

Daily routine

Normalmente, por la mañana me pego un madrugón porque tengo que ir al colegio. Me despierto a las siete, me levanto, me ducho y me visto antes de desayunar. Voy al colegio en autobús a las ocho y al llegar, charlo con mis amigos. Las clases empiezan a las nueve y tenemos ocho clases de cuarenta minutos al día. Vuelvo a casa a las cuatro y media, hago mis deberes, ceno con mi familia y después de cenar, suelo ver la tele en el salón o chatear por internet con mis amigos. Me acuesto sobre las diez.

Normally in the morning I have to get up really early because I have to go to school. I wake up at 7, I get up, shower and get dressed before having breakfast. I go to school by bus at 8 and when I arrive I chat to my friends. Lessons begin at 9 and we have 8 lessons of 40 minutes each per day. I go home at 4.30, do my homework, eat with my family and after eating I usually watch TV in the lounge or chat online with my friends. I go to bed around 10.

Daily routine weekend

El fin de semana, suelo levantarme más tarde que normalmente porque no tengo que ir al colegio. Desayuno sobre las once y salgo con mis amigos al parque o al centro comercial para ir de compras. Por la tarde suelo jugar al tenis en el polideportivo, y siempre cenamos juntos en familia. A veces vemos una película en Netflix o pasamos la tarde jugando a las cartas. Paso unas horas haciendo mis deberes, pero suelo dejarlos para el final.

At the weekend I get up later than usual because I don't have to go to school. I have breakfast around 11 and I go out with my friends to the park or the shopping mall to go shopping. In the afternoon I usually play tennis at the sports centre, and we always have dinner together as a family. Sometimes we watch a film on Netflix or we spend the evening playing cards. I spend a few hours doing my homework, but I usually leave it until the last minute.

This morning

Hoy me pegué un madrugón porque tuve que ir al colegio, me duché, me vestí y desayuné de prisa antes de irme. Siempre tengo prisa por la mañana. Fui al colegio en autobús y llegué a las ocho. Al llegar, charlé con mis amigos e hice un poco más revisión para mi examen oral de español.

Today I got up really early because I had to go to school, I showered, got dressed and had breakfast quickly before leaving. I am always in a hurry in the morning. I went to school by bus and arrived at 8. I chatted with my friends and did a bit more revision for my Spanish oral exam.

This evening

Al llegar a casa voy a relajarme antes de hacer mis deberes. Veré la tele e intentaré olvidar el estrés del día escolar. ¡Ojalá pudiera! Cenaré sobre las siete. Después charlaré con mis compañeros de clase en las redes sociales, porque soy adicto y no puedo prescindir de Facebook y Snapchat.

When I get home I'm going to relax before doing my homework. I will watch TV and I will try to forget the stress of the school day. If only I could! I will have dinner around 7. Afterwards I will chat with my school friends on social networks because I am addicted and I can't manage without Facebook and Snapchat.

What you would change about your routine

Si fuera posible, no haría deberes durante la semana. Cada tarde tengo que hacer dos horas de deberes y estoy siempre cansado y estresado. Además, me gustaría quedarme acostado hasta más tarde. Los científicos dicen que los jóvenes necesitan más sueño y estoy completamente de acuerdo. El colegio debería empezar al mediodía.

If it were possible, I wouldn't do homework during the week. Every evening I have to do two hours of homework and I am always tired and stressed. Also, I would like to stay in bed until later. Scientists say that young people need more sleep and I am completely in agreement. School should start at midday.

Helping at home

Para ayudar mis padres lavo los platos / el coche, arreglo mi dormitorio, paso la aspiradora, pongo / quito la mesa, preparo la comida y a veces limpio la cocina. No obstante, me cuesta hacerlo ahora porque los profes nos dan tantos deberes y paso mucho tiempo revisando para mis exámenes. SI tuviera menos deberes, haría más para ayudar.

To help my parents I wash the dishes / the car, I tidy my room, I hoover, I lay / clear the table, I cook meals and sometimes I clean the kitchen. However, I struggle to do it now because the teachers give us so much homework and I spend a lot of time revising for exams. If I had less homework I would do more to help.

Help at home yesterday

Ayer lavé los platos, puse la mesa y arreglé mi dormitorio. Habría hecho más si hubiera tenido el tiempo, pero los profes nos dan demasiados deberes.

Yesterday I washed the dishes, laid the table and tidied my room. I would have done more if I had had time, but the teachers give us too much homework.

Cooking at home

Por lo general, mi madre prepara la comida, pero cuando no está, lo hago yo. Me gusta cocinar, y si tuviera el tiempo haría más, pero los profes nos dan demasiados deberes.

In general, my mother cooks the meals, but when she's not there, I do it. I like cooking, and if I had the time I would do more, but the teachers give us too much homework.

Plans for next weekend with family

El fin de semana que viene, me gustaría hacer ciclismo con mi padre porque nos gusta pasar tiempo al aire libre. Por la tarde voy a ir de compras con mi madre. Después iremos al cine para ver la nueva película de James Bond porque nos encantan las películas de acción. Antes de volver a casa cenaremos en un restaurante y discutiremos la película. Al llegar a casa me acostaré y dormiré como un tronco.

Next weekend I'd like to go cycling with my dad because we like spending time in the fresh air. In the afternoon I'm going to go shopping with my mother. Afterwards we will go to the cinema to see the new Bond film because we love action films. Before going home, we will have dinner in a restaurant and discuss the film. When I get home I will go to bed and sleep like a log.

Recent family activity

El fin de semana pasado fuimos al parque para pasear al perro, fuimos de compras y después volvimos a casa para comer. Por la tarde fuimos a visitar a mis abuelos que viven cerca de nosotros, tomamos té y comimos pasteles deliciosos. Al volver decidimos ver una película de acción. Me acosté a las once y dormí como un tronco.

Last weekend we went to the park to walk the dog, we went shopping and then we went home to eat. In the afternoon we went to visit my grandparents who live near us, we had tea and ate delicious cakes. When we got back (on returning) we decided to watch an action film. I went to bed at 11 and slept like a log.

HOME AND ABROAD

Describe your town

Tengo suerte porque vivo en Londres desde hace diez años y es la mejor ciudad del mundo. Lo que más me gusta es que hay un montón de cosas que hacer. Se puede ir al cine, al teatro, a restaurantes, a museos, y hay tiendas, polideportivos y parques donde se puede jugar al tenis o al futbol. Suelo ir al cine todos los fines de semana porque me encantan las películas. Lo que no me gusta es que hay mucho tráfico. Si hubiera menos tráfico, estaría feliz.

I'm lucky because I've been living in London for ten years and it's the best city in the world. What I like most is that there is a lot to do. You can go to the cinema, to the theatre, to restaurants, to museums, and there are shops, sports centres, parks where you can play tennis or football. I usually go to the cinema every weekend because I love films. If there was less traffic I would be happy.

Recent outing in town

El fin de semana pasado fui con ……. a Londres para ir de compras. Tuve que comprar un regalo para mi madre para su cumpleaños. Al llegar al centro, compramos muchísima ropa, y después comimos en una pizzería. ¡Qué deliciosa! Lo malo fue que casi olvidé de comprar un regalo para mi madre. Por suerte hay una tienda cerca de mi casa donde se venden libros interesantes sobre la naturaleza. Escogé un libro, lo compré y volví a casa. Le regalé el libro y a mi madre le gustó muchísimo.

Last weekend I went with …………… to London to go shopping. I had to buy a present for my mother for her birthday. On arriving in the centre, we bought a lot of clothes and afterwards we ate lunch in a pizzeria. How delicious! The bad thing was that I almost forgot to buy a present for my mother. Luckily there is a shop near my house where they sell interesting books on nature. I chose a book, bought it and went home. I gave her the book and my mother really loved it.

What is there for young people in your town?

Tengo suerte porque hay mucho que hacer para los jóvenes en mi barrio. Hay un polideportivo donde se puede hacer deporte y muchas distracciones divertidas. Suelo ir al cine, ir de compras, y jugar al tenis en el parque. Lo malo es que todo eso cuesta un ojo de la cara y no puedo permitírmelo. Sería perfecto si hubiera un lugar para los jóvenes donde reunirse, como un centro juvenil. Podríamos divertirnos sin gastarse un riñón.

I'm lucky because there is a lot to do for young people in my area. There is a sports centre where you can do sport and lots of fun activities. I usually go to the cinema, go shopping or play tennis in the park. The bad thing is that all this costs an arm and a leg and I can't afford it. It would be perfect if there was a place where young people could get together like a youth club. We could have fun without it costing a fortune.

What is there for tourists in your town?

No hay muchos sitios turísticos en mi barrio, pero tenemos suerte porque se puede fácilmente ir a Londres en tren para ver los monumentos, los museos y las galerías de arte. También se puede visitar el palacio de Buckingham donde vive la reina de Inglaterra. Si pudiera, visitaría los sitios turísticos más a menudo, pero cuesta un ojo de la cara y no puedo permitírmelo.

There aren't many tourist attractions in my area but we are lucky because you can easily go to London by train to see the sights, the museums and art galleries. You can also visit Buckingham Palace where the Queen of England lives. If I could I would visit the tourist attractions more often, but it costs a fortune and I can't afford it.

What would you do for young people in your town?

Lo que más me preocupa es que las actividades en mi barrio cuestan un ojo de la cara. Si pudiera cambiar algo en mi barrio, construiría un centro juvenil para que los jóvenes pudieran reunirse y divertirse sin gastarse un riñón. Además, pondría más rutas para ciclistas porque me encanta el ciclismo y las carreteras son demasiadas peligrosas para ciclistas debido al tráfico.

What worries me most is that the activities in my area cost a fortune. If I could change something in my area, I would build a youth centre so that young people could meet up and have fun without having to pay through the nose for it. Also, I would put in more cycle paths because I love cycling and the roads are too dangerous for cyclists due to the traffic.

Town and countryside

En mi opinión, la ciudad es mejor que el campo por muchas razones. Por ejemplo, se puede comer en restaurantes, ver películas, ir de compras y reunirse con amigos. Sobre todo, lo que más me gusta es el transporte público, porque no conduzco y tengo que coger el autobús para ir a ver a mis amigos. Si viviera en el campo, no podría ver mis amigos tan fácilmente. Sin embargo, hay ventajas de vivir en el campo. Es más tranquilo que la ciudad, es más relajante y se puede pasear al aire libre. En la ciudad, lo que más me preocupa es el tráfico y la contaminación del aire que van empeorando.

In my opinion the city is better than the countryside for many reasons. For example, you can eat in restaurants, watch films, go shopping and meet up with friends. What I like most is the public transport because I don't drive and I have to take the bus to go and see my friends. If I lived in the countryside I wouldn't be able to see my friends so easily. However, there are advantages of living in the countryside. It is quieter than the city, it's more relaxing and you can walk in the fresh air. In the city what bothers me most is the traffic and air pollution which are getting worse.

Where will you live in the future?

Cuando sea mayor, me gustaría seguir viviendo en Londres para que pudiera aprovechar todas las actividades y quedarme cerca de mis amigos. Viviré en una casa moderna y grande, bien equipado, con vistas bonitas. Es importante que haya suficiente espacio para fiestas porque me encanta bailar.

When I'm older I would like to continue living in London so I can make the most of all the activities and stay close to my friends. I will live in a modern, large, well-appointed house with pretty views. It is important that there is enough space for parties because I love dancing.

Weather in your region today

Hoy hace buen tiempo, pero es posible que más tarde llueva a mares. Vamos a ver.

Today the weather is good but it might pour with rain later. We shall see.

Seasonal changes in your region

En invierno hace más frio que en verano, pero el clima está cambiando, y ya no nieva en invierno como antes. La diferencia entre las estaciones está disminuyendo debido al calentamiento global.

In winter it is colder than in summer, but the climate is changing and it no longer snows in winter as it used to. The difference between the seasons is diminishing due to global warming.

Climate comparison with Spain

En España hace más calor que en Inglaterra, y por eso a los ingleses les encanta pasar las vacaciones allí. No obstante, en verano el calor puede ser insoportable. Aquí no hay tantas diferencias de clima durante el año. Llueve a mares todo el año.

In Spain it is hotter than in England and therefore the English love spending the holidays there. However, in summer the heat can be unbearable. Here there aren't such differences in weather during the year. It pours with rain all year round.

Climate change in your region

El clima va cambiando / está cambiando – no hay duda. Los coches y los aviones emiten gases tóxicos que suben a la atmosfera ycausan el calentamiento global y el efecto invernadero. Los mares suben y hay islas que empiezan a desaparecer. Hay más inundaciones y más tormentas que antes. Tenemos que actuar antes de que sea demasiado tarde para salvar el planeta.

The climate is changing – there's no doubt about it. Cars and planes emit toxic gases which go up into the atmosphere and cause global warming and the greenhouse effect. The sea levels are rising and there are islands which are beginning to disappear. There are more floods and more storms than before. We need to act before it's too late to save the planet.

Climate change solution

Tenemos que actuar lo antes posible para salvar el planeta. Tenemos que usar la bici en lugar del coche, viajar menos en avión y ahorrar energía para que los recursos naturales no se agoten. Deberíamos parar la destrucción de las selvas tropicales que producen el oxígeno que necesitamos. Deberíamos dejar de comer tanta carne porque las vacas tanto como los coches emiten gases tóxicos que causan el cambio climático.

We need to act as soon as possible to save the planet. We need to use bikes instead of the car, travel less by plane and save energy so that natural resources don't run out. We should stop the destruction of tropical forests which produce the oxygen we need. We should stop eating so much meat because the cows, just like the cars, give off toxic gases which cause climate change.

Transport in your region

Tengo suerte porque hay una buena red de transporte en mi barrio. Hay trenes, autobuses y el metro y se puede fácilmente desplazarse. Lo único es que las calles son ruidosas y hay demasiados atascos. Si hubiera más rutas para ciclistas pienso que no habría tanta contaminación del aire.

I'm lucky because there is a good public transport network in my area. There are trains, buses and the underground and you can get around easily. The only thing is that the streets are noisy and there are too many traffic jams. If there were more cycle paths, I think there wouldn't be so much air pollution.

Favourite transport

Mi transporte favorito es el avión, aunque sea malo para el medioambiente, porque es rápido, cómodo y se puede ver películas, comer, beber y leer durante el viaje. No me gusta el tren porque nunca encuentro un asiento. ¡Qué molesto!

My favourite transport is the plane, although it is bad for the environment, because it's fast, comfortable and you can watch films, eat, drink and read during the journey. I don't like trains because I never find a seat. How annoying!

Usual holidays

Tengo suerte porque todos los años suelo ir a España en avión con mi familia y nos alojamos en un hotel cerca de la playa durante dos semanas. Me encanta porque en mi opinión es el mejor país del mundo. Hace calor, la gente es simpática y la comida riquísima. Suelo pasar muchas horas relajándome y olvidando el estrés de mi vida. Juego al tenis todos los días, tomo el sol, nado en el mar y hago nuevos amigos. Me lo paso bomba.

I'm lucky because every year I go to Spain by plane with my family and we stay in a hotel near the beach for two weeks. I love it because in my opinion it is the best country in the world. It's hot, the people are nice and the food is delicious. I usually spend hours relaxing and forgetting the stress of my life. I play tennis every day, I sunbathe, swim in the sea and make new friends. I have a great time.

Last year's holiday

Tengo suerte porque hace un año, fui a ………………….. en …barco / coche / avión con …una amiga / unas amigas / un amigo / unos amigos / mi familia. Pasé ………………. días / semanas / meses relajándome. Nos alojamos en un hotel cerca de la playa. Tomé el sol, hice la equitación, jugué al tenis, nadé en el mar, visité monumentos históricos, descansé, leí libros, conocí a gente nueva,dormí mucho. Hice sol todos los días. Fue fenomenal.

¡Me lo pasé bomba!

I am lucky because a year ago I went to ....by boat / car / plane with a friend / with friends / with my family. I spent .... days /weeks / months relaxing. We stayed in a hotel near the beach. I sunbathed, went horseriding, played tennis, swam in the sea, visited historical sites, relaxed, read books, met new people, slept a lot. It was sunny every day. It was amazing. I had a great time.

Purchases on hoilday

Para mi mejor amigo compré una camiseta roja para su cumpleaños. Si hubiera podido, le habría comprado algo más interesante pero no podía permitírmelo.

I bought a red T-shirt for my best friend's birthday. If I could have I would have bought him something more interesting but I couldn't afford it.

Future holiday

El año que viene / cuando haya terminado mis exámenes, iré a Grecia con mi familia y unos amigos. Nos alojaremos en un hotel cerca de la playa y vamos a jugar al tenis todos los días. Tomaré el sol, nadaré en el mar y descansaré porque tendré que relajarme después de los exámenes. Espero con ganas las vacaciones.

Next year / when I have finished my exams, I will go to Greece with my family and some friends. We will stay in a hotel near the beach and we are going to play tennis every day. I will sunbathe, swim in the sea and relax because I will need to rest after the exams. I am looking forward to it.

Ideal holiday

Si fuera rica iría a Francia. Tengo ganas de ir el año que viene con mi mejor amiga para unas semanas. Nos alojaríamos en un hotel de cinco estrellas cerca de la playa. Pasaríamos todos los días relajándonos, jugando al tenis, nadando en el mar y tomando el sol. Haríamos nuevos amigos, probaríamos los platos típicos de laregión y compraríamos recuerdos. Haría sol todos los días. ¡Qué perfecto!

If I was rich I would go to France. I would like to go next year with my best friend for a few weeks. We would stay in a five-star hotel near the beach. We would spend every day relaxing, playing tennis, swimming in the sea and sunbathing. We would make new friends, we would try the local dishes and buy souvenirs. It would be sunny every day. How perfect!

Holidays with parents or friends?

Lo bueno de ir de vacaciones con mis padres es que pagan todo y no tengo que pensar en nada. Nos alojamos en hoteles lujosos y comimos los platos típicos de la región. Lo malo es que tengo que visitar sitios turísticos que no me interesan. ¡Qué aburrido! Tengo ganas de ir de vacaciones con mis amigos para que pueda aprovechar la libertad y la falta de museos.

The good thing about going on holiday with my parents is that they pay for everything and I don't have to think about anything. We stay in luxury hotels and we eat local food. The bad thing is that I have to visit tourist sites which don't interest me. How boring! I would like to go on holiday with my friends so that I can make the most of the freedom and the lack of museums.

Importance of holidays

Las vacaciones son importantes por muchas razones. Primero tenemos que relajarnos después del trabajo cuando hemos currado un montón. También es importante conocer la cultura de los países extranjeros para que podamos tener un mejor entendimiento sobre la gente del mundo. Además, se puede aprovechar la oportunidad de aprender nuevos deportes y probar nuevas actividades por primera vez.

Holidays are important for many reasons. Firstly, we need to relax after work when we have been working our socks off. Also, it's important to get to know the culture of foreign countries so that we can have a better understanding of the people of the world. Moreover, you can learn new sports and take the opportunity to try new activities for the first time.

Camping

No me gusta hacer camping porque no es cómodo. Prefiero dormir en mi cama.

I don't like camping because it's not comfortable. I prefer sleeping in my bed.

Festivals in England

No hay muchas fiestas in Inglaterra. La única fiesta que celebramos en nuestra familia es la Navidad, mientras que en España hay un montón de fiestas durante todo el año. La mayoría son religiosas, pero también hay fiestas divertidas como la Tomatina cerca de Valencia, donde los participantes se arrojan tomates los unos a los otros. Si solo tuviéramos batallas de tomates aquí en Inglaterra. Claro que tenemos fiestas de arte y de música como en todos los países. No obstante, las fiestas de música cuestan un ojo de la cara.

There aren't many festivals in England. The only festival we celebrate in our family is Christmas, whereas in Spain there are loads of festivals all year round. Most of them are religious but there are also fun festivals like the Tomatina near Valencia where they throw tomatoes at each other. If only we had tomato battles here in England... Of course, we have art and music festivals as all countries do. However, music festivals cost a fortune.

Last Christmas

El año pasado, mis abuelos vinieron a vernos y pasamos el día juntos, comiendo, bebiendo, hablando y jugando. Recibí un montón de regalos. ¡Qué bueno! Después de una comida riquísima vimos la televisión y mi abuelo se durmió en el sofá. Antes de acostarnos jugamos a las cartas, pero mi padre tocó el piano y tuvimos que taparnos los oídos.

Last year my grandparents came to see us and we spent the day together, eating, drinking, talking and playing. I received loads of presents. How great! After a delicious meal we watched television and my grandfather fell asleep on the sofa. Before going to bed we played cards but my father played the piano and we had to block our ears.

Next Christmas

Este año mis abuelos van a venir a vernos, y pasaremos el día juntos, comiendo, bebiendo, hablando y jugando. Recibiré un montón de regalos. ¡Qué bueno! Después de una comida riquísima veremos la televisión y mi abuelo se dormirá en el sofá. Antes de acostarnos jugaremos a las cartas, mi padre tocará el piano y tendremos que taparnos los oídos.

Next year my grandparents will come to see us and we will spend the day together, eating, drinking, talking and playing. I will get loads of presents. How great! After a delicious meal we will watch television and my grandfather will fall asleep on the sofa. Before going to bed we will play cards, my father will play the piano and we will have to block our ears.

EDUCATION AND WORK

Describe your school

Mi colegio se llama .... y está en .... cerca de .... Tengo suerte porque es el mejor colegio del mundo y voy allí desde hace cinco años. Lo que más me gusta es que es grande, con partes antiguas y partes modernas. Hay aulas, laboratorios, un comedor, un campo deportivo donde se puede jugar al futbol, y una biblioteca donde paso muchas horas trabajando, pero no hay piscina. Si hubiera una piscina y un cine, sería perfecto.

My school is called .... and it is in .... near .... I'm lucky because it's the best school in the world and I've been going there for 5 years. What I like most is that it's big with some old parts and some modern parts. There are classrooms, laboratories, a dining room, a sports field where you can play football and a library where I spend many hours working, but there isn't a pool. If there was a pool and a cinema it would be perfect.

Likes and dislikes about school

Me gusta mi colegio porque tengo muchos amigos, pero lo que no me gusta es que los profes nos dan demasiados deberes. También, si hubiera una piscina / un cine, estaría contentísimo. Si pudiera cambiar algo, cambiaría el uniforme porque es incómodo y feo. Estoy harto de él.

I like my school because I have lots of friends but what I don't like is that the teachers give us too much homework. Also if there was a pool / a cinema I would be very happy. If I could change something I would change the uniform because it's uncomfortable and ugly. I'm sick of it.

School day

Las clases empiezan a las nueve y terminan a las cuatro. Tenemos seis clases al día y cada clase dura una hora. Durante el recreo, juego con mis amigos y como un bocadillo. A menudo voy a un club

durante la hora de comer. A veces voy al colegio andando, pero normalmente voy en coche y vuelvo en tren. Suelo hacer dos horas de deberes por la tarde.

Lessons begin at 9 and finish at 4. We have 6 lessons a day and each one lasts an hour. During break time I play with my friends and eat a sandwich. I often go to a club at lunchtime. Sometimes I walk to school but normally I go to school by car and come back by train. I usually do two hours of homework in the evening.

Subjects

Estoy estudiando el francés, el español, el dibujo, el latín, el inglés, el deporte, las ciencias, las matemáticas, la música, la historia y la geografía. Mi asignatura favorita es ....porque el profe es simpático y saco buenas notas. No me gusta el latín porque es difícil, el profe es aburrido y el profe nos da demasiados deberes.

I am studying French, Spanish, art, Latin, English, sport, sciences, maths, music, history and geography. My favourite subject is ..... because the teacher is nice and I get good marks. I don't like Latin because it's difficult, the teacher is boring and the teacher gives us too much homework.

Describe a teacher

Mi profe de español es mi profe favorito por supuesto. Se llama …………….. y tiene el pelo rubio y los ojos azules. Lo que más me gusta es que es el profe más inteligente del colegio, me hace reír y al mismo tiempo siempre explica todo muy lentamente para que pueda comprender lo que hacemos.

My Spanish teacher is my favourite teacher of course. He / she is called …………... and he / she has blonde hair and blue eyes. What I like most is that he / she is the most intelligent teacher in the school, makes me laugh and at the same time always explains everything very slowly so I can understand what we are doing.

Describe your uniform

Tenemos que llevar un uniforme: [una falda negra, una camisa blanca, pantalones negros, una chaqueta negra, zapatos negros, calcetines o medias, una corbata y un jersey]. Si pudiera cambiar algo, cambiaría el uniforme porque es incómodo y feo. Estoy harto de él.

We have to wear a uniform – [a black skirt, a white shirt, black trousers, a black jacket, black shoes, socks or tights, a tie and a jumper]. If I could change something, I would change the uniform because it's uncomfortable and ugly. I'm sick of it.

Opinion of uniform

Claro que hay ventajas de llevar un uniforme. No tienes que pensar en lo que vas a poner por la mañana y no hay presión de vestirse de manera elegante, de moda. Todos se parecen y así se puede evitar el acoso escolar. No obstante, en mi colegio, si pudiera cambiar algo, cambiaría el uniforme porque es incómodo y feo. Estoy harto de él.

Of course there are advantages to wearing a uniform. You don't have to think about what you are going to wear in the morning and there is no pressure to dress in a fashionable way. Everyone looks the same and in this way you can avoid bullying in schools. However, if I could change something in my school I would change the uniform because it's uncomfortable and ugly. I'm sick of it.

Yesterday at school

Ayer fui al cole en autobús y al llegar, charlé con mis amigos. Las clases empezaron a las nueve y tuve cinco clases de cuarenta minutos antes de la comida. Durante el recreo a las diez y veinte, comí una galleta y jugué al baloncesto. Durante la hora de comer, comimos en el comedor y después fui al club de teatro porque es mi pasatiempo favorito. Las clases terminaron a las cuatro y volví a casa para cenar y hacer mis deberes.

Yesterday I went to school by bus and when I arrived I chatted with my friends. Lessons began at 9 and I had 5 classes of 40 minutes each before lunch. During break at 10.20 I ate a biscuit and played basketball. During the lunch hour we ate in the canteen and afterwards I went to drama club because it's my favourite hobby. Lessons finished at 4 and I went home to have dinner and do my homework.

Opinion of homework

Aunque sean útiles para comprender lo que hemos aprendido en el colegio, los deberes me molestan porque los profes nos dan demasiados. Yo tengo dos horas de deberes al día y estoy siempre agotado. Si no los hubiera, por lo menos durante la semana, sería mucho mejor.

Although it's useful for understanding what we have learnt in class, homework annoys me because the teachers give us too much. I have two hours of homework per day and I'm always exhausted! If we didn't have any, at least during the week, it would be much better.

What you would change at school

Si pudiera cambiar algo, cambiaría el uniforme porque es incómodo y feo. Estoy harto de él. También no habría deberes durante la semana. Lo importante es que los estudiantes estén totalmente despiertos en clase para que puedan estudiar y aprender. Sería todavía mejor si las clases empezaran más tarde porque, según los científicos, los jóvenes necesitan más sueño por la mañana.

If I could change something, I would change the uniform because it's uncomfortable and ugly. I'm sick of it. Also, there wouldn't be any homework during the week. The important thing is that students are wide awake in class so that they can study and learn. It would be even better if lessons began later because, according to scientists, young people need more sleep in the morning.

School rules

Las reglas son bastante estrictas. Por ejemplo, no se puede usar el móvil durante las clases; no se puede comer chicle tampoco. Si charlamos, los profes se enfadan. Ayer gané un castigo por hablar en clase y tuve que quedarme en el colegio hasta las cinco de la tarde. El maquillaje está prohibido pero las chicas lo ponen de todas formas.

The rules are quite strict. For example, you can't use your phone during lessons; you can't chew gum either. If we chat, the teachers get cross. Yesterday I got a detention for talking in class and had to stay at school until 5pm. Make-up isn't allowed but the girls wear it anyway.

Ideal school

Mi colegio ideal sería grande y moderno y estaría cerca de mi casa. Habría un polideportivo, donde pasaríamos muchísimas horas jugando al baloncesto, habría una piscina enorme y un cine. No habría uniforme y los profes no darían deberes durante la semana. Las clases empezarían al mediodía porque según los científicos, los jóvenes necesitan más sueño por la mañana. ¡Qué perfecto!

My ideal school would be big and modern and would be near my house. There would be a sports centre where we would spend many hours playing basketball, an enormous pool and a cinema. There wouldn't be a uniform and the teachers wouldn't give homework. Lessons would begin at midday because according to scientists, young people need more sleep in the morning. How perfect!

Primary school

Cuando era joven iba a una escuela primaria cerca de mi casa. Los profes eran simpáticos y no nos daban tantos deberes que ahora. ¡Qué bueno! Había un gran jardín donde solíamos jugar durante el recreo. Lo malo era que no me gustaba la comida escolar porque nos daban demasiadas verduras.

When I was young, I went to a primary school near my house. The teachers were nice and didn't give us as much homework as they do now. How great! There was a big garden where we used to play at breaktime. The bad thing was that I didn't like the school dinners because they gave us too many vegetables.

Spanish and English schools

Parece que los colegios españoles son menos estrictos que los colegios ingleses. No tienen uniforme y el ambiente en el colegio es mucho más agradable porque los alumnos no tienen miedo de los profes. Mi amiga española me dijo que no tiene exámenes cada año como nosotros. ¡Qué suerte! Estoy tan envidioso de los estudiantes españoles. Lo malo es que, al fin y al cabo, parece que los estudiantes españoles no tienen tanto éxito como nosotros después del colegio, y el desempleo va aumentando entre los jóvenes españoles.

It seems that Spanish schools are less strict than English schools. They don't have uniform and the atmosphere in the school is much nicer because the pupils are not scared of the teachers. My Spanish friend told me that she doesn't have exams every year like we do. How lucky! I am so jealous of the Spanish students. The bad thing is that at the end of the day, it seems that Spanish students are less successful then us after school and unemployment is rising amongst

Spanish young people.

Future education

El año que viene voy a seguir estudiando el inglés, la historia y las matemáticas porque son mis asignaturas favoritas. Dejaré las ciencias porque me aburren. Trabajaré duro para que pueda ir a una buena universidad, donde espero estudiar el derecho.

Next year I am going to carry on studying English, history and maths because they are my favourite subjects. I will give up sciences because they bore me. I will work hard so I can go to a good university, where I hope to study law.

Part-time job / work experience

El año pasado pasé una semana trabajando en un colegio y me gustó mucho, pero he currado un montón y no gané nada. Ahora tengo un trabajo a tiempo parcial desde hace dos meses en un restaurante en mi barrio que se llama Pizza Mama y es harina de otro costal. Trabajo el sábado de las dos hasta las seis de la tarde. Trabajo en la cocina, lavando los platos y preparando las verduras y las ensaladas. En el restaurante mismo, pongo las mesas y sirvo a los clientes. Lo que más me gusta es el dinero porque los clientes siempre me dan propinas enormes. ¡Me lo paso bomba!

Last year I spent a week working in a school and I liked it a lot but I worked my socks off and earned nothing. Now I have had a part time job for the past two months in a restaurant in my area called Pizza Mama and it's something else entirely. I work on Saturdays from 2 till 6. I work in the kitchen washing dishes and preparing vegetables and salads. In the restaurant itself I lay the tables and serve clients. What I like most is the money because the clients always give huge tips. I have a great time!

Future job

No sé exactamente qué voy a hacer cuando sea mayor. Lo importante es que sea interesante. Me gustaría hacerme profe de historia porque es mi asignatura favorita y los profes tienen suerte porque no trabajan durante el verano.

I don't know exactly what I want to do when I'm older. The important thing is that it is interesting. I would like to become a history teacher because it's my favourite subject, and teachers are lucky because they don't work during the summer.

Ideal job

Si pudiera elegir, y si no tuviera que ganar dinero, iría a un país del tercero mundo para trabajar como médico voluntario. Hay millones de personas que sufren debido a las guerras y al terrorismo y me gustaría hacer algo para ayudarles.

If I could choose and if I didn't have to earn money I would go to a third world country to do voluntary work as a doctor. There are millions of people suffering because of wars and terrorism and I'd like to do something to help them.

MODERN WORLD AND ENVIRONMENT

Nowadays what are the biggest environmental problems?

Hoy en día, hay un montón de problemas medioambientales. Lo que más me preocupa es la contaminación. Los coches, las fábricas, y la industria emiten gases tóxicos que suben en la atmosfera y causan la contaminación del aire, el calentamiento global y el efecto invernadero. Por consiguiente, las temperaturas aumentan, se funden los casquetes polares y el nivel de los mares va aumentando. Me da miedo por las generaciones futuras debido a los problemas de calentamiento global.

Nowadays, there are lots of environmental problems. What worries me most is pollution. Cars, factories and industry emit toxic gases, which go into the atmosphere and cause air pollution, global warming and the greenhouse effect. Consequently, the temperatures increase, the polar ice caps melt and the sea level rises. I am afraid for the future generations due to the problems of global warming.

Why protect the environment?

A pesar de nuestros esfuerzos, nuestro planeta está a punto de morir. ¡Qué desastre! Si no hacemos nada, la situación solo empeorará, asi que hace falta que todos luchemos por el medioambiente. Es imposible cerrar los ojos ante los problemas asociados con el calentamiento global.

In spite of our efforts, our planet is about to die. What a disaster! If we do not do anything, the situation will only get worse, so we must all fight for the environment. It is impossible to close our eyes to the problems associated with global warming.

Recycling

Creo que la protección del planeta debería ser la responsabilidad de cada uno. Lo más importante es actuar, incluso el acto más sencillo marca la diferencia. En mi familia no dejamos en nuestro empeño de reciclar todo; el cartón, el papel, las botellas, el plástico, el vidrio, las latas y el embalaje.

I believe that the protection of the planet should be everybody's responsibility. The most important thing is to act, even the smallest act can make a difference. In my family we try our best to recycle everything; cardboard, paper, bottles, plastic, glass, tins and packaging.

The importance of recycling

Hoy en día la situación medioambiental es muy preocupada. Es imprescindible que reciclemos todo lo posible para que los recursos naturales no se agoten y para que nuestros hijos puedan vivir en un mundo limpio.

Nowadays the situation in relation to the environment is very worrying. It is essential that we recycle everything possible so our natural resources don't run out and so that our children can live in a clean world.

What do you do for the environment at home?

Hago lo que puedo para proteger el medioambiente. Por ejemplo, me ducho en lugar de bañarme para ahorrar agua, apago las luces para ahorrar electricidad, y cierro los grifos cuando no se usan. Además, no dejamos en nuestro empeño de reciclar el cartón, el papel, el plástico y el vidrio. Aprovecho el transporte público en lugar de viajar en coche, y compro productos ecológicos.

I do what I can to protect the environment. For example, I shower instead of taking a bath to save water, I turn off the lights to save electricity and the taps when I'm not using them. Also we do our best to recycle cardboard, paper, plastic and glass. I make the most of public transport instead of travelling by car and I buy green products.

What do you do for the environment at school?

En colegio hacemos todo lo posible para proteger el medioambiente. Hay una papelera de reciclaje en todas las aulas, apagamos las luces cuando salimos de las aulas para ahorrar electricidad y los profesores nos animan a utilizar el transporte público en lugar de un coche para viajar al colegio porque el acto más sencillo puede marcar la diferencia.

At school we do everything possible to protect the environment. There is a recycling bin in every classroom, we turn off the lights when we leave the classrooms to save electricity, and the teachers encourage us to use public transport instead of a car to travel to school, because the simplest act can make a difference.

What should we be doing for the environment?

Es imprescindible que todos luchemos por el medioambiente para que los recursos naturales no se agoten y para que nuestros hijos puedan vivir en un mundo limpio. Deberíamos seguir haciendo todo lo posible porque el acto más sencillo puede marcar la diferencia. Por ejemplo, deberíamos ducharnos en lugar de bañarnos para ahorrar agua, apagar las luces cuando salimos de un cuarto para ahorrar electricidad, y reciclar todo lo posible y aprovechar el transporte público en vez de viajar en coche para reducir la contaminación del aire.

It is essential that we all fight for the environment so that natural resources don't run out and so that our children can live in a clean world. We should continue to do everything possible because the simplest act can make a difference. For example, we should shower instead of having baths to save water, we should turn off the lights when we leave a room to save electricity, recycle everything possible and we should make the most of public transport instead of travelling by car in order to reduce air pollution.

What should the government do for the environment?

Es fundamental que tengamos leyes para proteger el medioambiente. Por ejemplo, opino que el gobierno debería limitar el número de coches en las carreteras y debería construir más rutas para ciclistas para que podamos usar bicicletas en lugar del coche. Si hubiera más rutas para ciclistas pienso que no habría tanta contaminación del aire.

It's fundamental that we have laws to protect the environment. For example, I think that the government should limit the number of cars on the roads and should construct more cycle routes so that we can use bicycles instead of cars. If there were more cycle routes I think that there wouldn't be as much air pollution.

The causes of poverty in the world

Lo que más me preocupa es la pobreza. La mitad del planeta vive en la miseria y la otra mitad tira comida en buen estado. La pobreza se extiende cada vez más, a causa de las guerras, del clima que va cambiando y de conflictos políticos. Las ciudades del mundo están superpobladas, y en poco tiempo habrá grandes problemas de vivienda. Los conflictos mundiales obligan a millones de personas a huir la hambruna y la persecución. Actualmente, la crisis de refugiados en Europa es una situación humanitaria critica. Incluso en Inglaterra, mucha gente vive por debajo del umbral de la pobreza y la situación va empeorando.

Hay un montón de familias donde nadie ha tenido un empleo en generaciones. El gobierno debería hacer más para ayudar los niños de estas familias para que puedan acceder a la educación y las oportunidades que merecen.

What worries me most is poverty. Half the world is living in poverty and the other half is throwing away decent food. Poverty is becoming more and more widespread because of wars, a changing climate and political conflict. The cities of the world are overpopulated, and in a short time there will be big problems with living space. World conflicts force millions of people to flee hunger and persecution. Currently the refugee crisis in Europe is a critical humanitarian situation. Even in England lots of people live below the poverty line and the situation is getting worse. There are lots of families where nobody has had a job for generations. The government should do more to encourage the children of these families so that they can access the education and the opportunities they deserve.

Importance of the news

Las noticias pueden tener una gran influencia positiva. Son informativas sobre temas actuales y todos tenemos que saber lo que pasa en el mundo. Sin embargo, lo importante es que las noticias sean imparciales, porque los medios son tan poderosos hoy en día. Es imprescindible que tengamos leyes para que los medios no puedan mentir y manipular sus lectores, como lo hacen en otros países del mundo.

The news can have a major positive influence. It informs us on current issues and we all need to know what is happening in the world. However, what is important is that the news is unbiased because the media is so powerful today. It is essential that we have laws so that the media cannot lie and manipulate its readers as they do in other countries in the world

Do you watch the news?

Las noticias me interesan y si tuviera más tiempo, leería un periódico todos los días, pero los profes nos dan demasiados deberes y me cuesta estar al día. Tengo la aplicación de la BBC en mi móvil que me avisa cuando pasa algo importante en el mundo, y si quiero saber más, hago clic en el icono para abrirlo.

I am interested in the news and if I had more time I would read a paper every day, but the teachers give us too much homework and I find it hard to stay up to date. I have the BBC app on my phone which tells me when something important happens in the world and if I want to know more, I click on the icon to open it.

What's in the news at the moment?

En cuanto a los titulares, a menudo tratan del medioambiente. Los problemas medioambientales van empeorando. Debido al cambio climático hay más terremotos, tormentas e inundaciones que matan a muchísimas personas. También, la situación política en Europa sigue siendo delicada, debido a la subida de sentimientos antiinmigrantes. Mucha gente piensa que la inmigración provoca el terrorismo porque hemos abierto las puertas a todos, incluso los criminales. Pero al mismo tiempo, tenemos que hacer frente a la crisis humanitaria. ¡Qué complicado!

As far as the headlines are concerned, they are often about the environment. Environmental problems are getting worse. Due to climate change there are more earthquakes, storms and floods which kill a lot of people. Also, the political situation in Europe continues to be delicate due to the rise of anti-immigration feeling. Lots of people think that immigration causes terrorism because we have opened the doors to everyone, including criminals. But at the same time we need to face the humanitarian crisis. How complex!

Do you watch TV?

Si, veo las telenovelas todos los días para relajarme, y porque me hacen reír y los vemos juntos, mis hermanos y yo. Además, nunca me pierdo los programas de deportes, especialmente los partidos de futbol. Veo las noticias de vez en cuando porque me informan y me interesan mucho. Si tuviera más tiempo vería más programas, pero los profes nos dan demasiados deberes.

Yes, I watch soap operas every day to relax and because they make me laugh and I watch them together with my brothers. In addition, I never miss sports programmes, especially football matches. I watch the news from time to time because it is informative and interesting. If I had more time I would watch more programmes but the teachers give us too much homework.

Young people and TV

Creo que si vemos la televisión corremos el riesgo de pasar demasiadas horas encerrados en casa. Puede crear adicción en algunas personas que pierden el control de las horas que pasan delante de la pequeña pantalla y por consiguiente pierden la capacidad de comunicar cara a cara. Sin embargo, pienso que ver la televisión es mejor que los videojuegos y las redes sociales porque los documentales pueden ser una herramienta educativa ya que permiten que los jóvenes sean conscientes de problemas sociales y globales.

I believe that if we watch television we risk spending too much time stuck at home. It can create addiction in some people who lose control of the hours that they spend in front of the small screen and consequently lose the capacity to communicate face to face. However, I think that watching television is better than video games and social networks because documentaries can be an educational tool as they make young people aware of social and global problems.

Advantages of TV

Para empezar, la televisión puede ser una herramienta educativa dado que hay muchos programas que ayudan a los niños a aprender. Por ejemplo, los documentales tienen una influencia positiva puesto que no solo nos divierten, sino también nos enseñan. Además, la televisión puede ser una diversión inocua y puede ayudar a la gente a descansar y desconectar de la rutina diaria. Opino que la televisión es un buen medio de relajarse después de un día estresante en el colegio.

Firstly, television can be an educational tool because there are many programmes which help children to learn. For example, documentaries have a positive influence because not only do they entertain us but also teach us. In addition, television can be a harmless hobby and can help people to rest and disconnect from their daily routine. I think that television is a good way to relax after a stressful day at school.

Disadvantages of TV

Si vemos la televisión corremos el riesgo de pasar demasiadas horas encerrados en casa. Puede crear adicción en algunas personas que pierden el control de las horas que pasan delante de la pequeña pantalla y por consiguiente pierden la capacidad de comunicar cara a cara. Además, según mucha gente, hay cada vez más violencia en la televisión, particularmente en los dibujos animados que están dirigidos a los niños. ¡Qué horror! Los espectadores de las pelis de acción se están insensibilizando a la violencia y hoy en día los jóvenes ya no están impactados por imágenes chocantes.

I believe that if we watch television we risk spending too much time stuck at home. It can create addiction in some people who lose control of the hours that they spend in front of the small screen and consequently lose the capacity to communicate face to face. Also, according to many people, there is more and more violence on television, particularly in cartoons aimed at children. How awful! People who watch action films are becoming desensitized and the young are no longer affected by shocking images.

Advertising

Hoy en día podemos ver y oír la publicidad en todas partes. Vaya donde vaya, hay carteles o anuncios publicitarios, viajando en el coche vemos vallas publicitarias en las calles y a la vez escuchamos en la radio avisos publicitaros. Al leer un periódico o una revista encontramos anuncios publicitarios y mientras navegamos por Internet observamos anuncios por todas partes.

Nowadays we can see and hear advertising everywhere. Wherever you go there are signs or adverts, travelling by car we can see billboards in the streets and at the same time listen to adverts on the radio. When reading a newspaper or magazine we find adverts and while we surf the Internet we see adverts everywhere.

Positives of advertising

La principal ventaja de la publicidad es promover y dar a conocer al público un producto, e informar al consumidor sobre los beneficios que presenta el producto. Es la manera más efectiva de aumentar el número de ventas de un producto, sobre todo hoy en día mediante las redes sociales. Además, aunque pueda ser molesto, la publicidad es la razón por la cual las redes sociales permanecen gratis.

The main advantage of advertising is to promote and publicise a product to the public, and to inform the consumer about the benefits. It is the most effective method of increasing the sales of a product, especially today by using social networks. Also, although it can be annoying, advertising is the reason social networks are free.

Negatives of advertising

La publicidad a muchas veces nos engaña para que compremos productos o servicios, y puede provocar la avidez. Los anuncios que promueven la comida basura y los cigarrillos deberían ser prohibidos porque promueven productos que son malos para la salud y pueden causar enfermedades graves como el cáncer. Además, la publicidad puede tener una influencia peligrosa en los jóvenes que piensan que deberían ser tan delgados y guapos como los modelos que ven en los anuncios, en la tele, donde sea.

La presión puede causar trastornos alimentarios como anorexia.

Advertising often deceives us to make us buy products or services and can provoke greed in people. I think that adverts promoting junk food and cigarettes should be banned because they promote products which are bad for your health and can cause serious illnesses like cancer. Also, advertising can have a dangerous influence on young people who think they should be as thin and gorgeous as the models they see on the adverts, on TV, wherever. The pressure can cause eating disorders like anorexia.

Cinema

Me gustan las películas y el cine. Los domingos por la mañana, aunque tenga poco dinero, voy al cine y mi hermana mayor me acompaña. Antes de ir, busco las mejores películas en internet. A mi hermana le gustan las películas de amor mientras que yo prefiero las películas de ciencia ficción y de acción. Si tuviera más dinero iría todos los días, pero cuesta un ojo de la cara y no puedo permitírmelo.

I like films and cinema. On Sunday mornings, although I don't have much money, I go to the cinema with my older sister. Before going I find the best films on the Internet. My sister likes romantic films whilst I prefer science fiction and action films. If I had more money, I'd go every day but it costs an arm and a leg and I can't afford it.

What films do you like?

En cuanto al cine, no me gustan nada las películas románticas. Prefiero las películas de acción, sobre todo las pelis de James Bond porque son emocionantes y no me aburren. Hay un montón de efectos especiales y juegan muchísimas estrellas de cine. Suelo ir al cine todos los fines de semana con mis amigos. Si tuviera más dinero iría todos los días, pero cuesta un ojo de la cara y no puedo permitírmelo.

As for cinema, I do not like romantic films at all. I prefer action films, above all James Bond films because they are exciting and they don't bore me. There are loads of special effects and lots of movie stars acting in them. I usually go to the cinema every weekend with my friends. If I had more money, I'd go every day but it costs an arm and a leg and I can't afford it.

Cinema or TV?

Prefiero el cine porque a mí me encantan las pelis de ciencia ficción y prefiero verlas en la pantalla grande. Disfruto mucho más de los efectos especiales, de la banda sonora y de los efectos visuales. Además, cuando ves una película en casa, hay un montón de distracciones, y siempre hay alguien que quiere cambiar de canal.

I prefer the cinema because I love science fiction films and I prefer to watch them on the big screen. I enjoy the effects, the soundtrack and the visual effects much more. Also when you watch a film at home there are loads of distractions and there is always someone who wants to change channel.

The last film you saw

Acabo de ver Titanic y fue estupendo. Trata de dos jóvenes amantes que cruzan sus destinos en el viaje inaugural del crucero Titanic. Pero cuando el crucero choca con un iceberg en el gélido Océano Atlántico Norte, su apasionado encuentro amoroso se convierte en una desesperada carrera por sobrevivir. No me sorprende que es la película de más éxito de todos los tiempos.

I have just watched Titanic and it was great. It is about two young lovers whose destinies cross on the inaugural journey of the cruise ship Titanic. But when the ship hits an iceberg in the frozen North Atlantic their passionate encounter becomes a desperate race to survive. It doesn't surprise me that it's the most successful film of all time.

Mobile phones – do you have one and why?

Tengo suerte porque tengo mi propio móvil desde hace cinco años y lo uso para mandar mensajes, hablar con mis amigos en las redes sociales, escuchar música, sacar fotos y navegar por internet. Lo que más me gusta es que los móviles hacen la comunicación más sencilla, pero si tuviera más dinero, compraría el ultima modelo porque mi móvil es fuera de moda. No puedo prescindir del móvil. Soy adicto.

I am lucky because I have had my own mobile for 5 years and I use it to send messages, talk to my friends on social networks, listen to music, take photos and go on the internet. What I like most is that mobiles make communication much easier but if I had more money, I would buy the latest model because my mobile is out-dated. I could not survive without my phone. I am addicted to it.

Young people and mobile phones

A los jóvenes les gustan los móviles porque son extremadamente útiles, para chatear con amigos en las redes sociales, descargar y escuchar música, sacar fotos y navegar por la red. Muchas jóvenes no podrían prescindir del móvil y su adicción puede ser peligroso.

Young people like mobile phones because they are extremely useful, to chat to friends on social networks, download and listen to music, take photos and surf the web. Most young people couldn't manage without a mobile and their addiction can be dangerous.

Advantages of technology

1. No cabe duda de que los móviles y el internet hacen la comunicación mucho más sencilla. La mayor ventaja es que se puede comunicar con personas de todas partes del mundo.
2. Podemos informarnos sobre cualquier cosa cuando queramos.
3. Me ayuda con mis deberes.
4. La tecnología permite que este siempre en contacto con todos y aprovecho las aplicaciones como Whatsapp y Snapchat para comunicar con mis amigos todo el tiempo.

5. Me pongo al día con las aplicaciones de noticias, que me avisan cuando pasa algo importante.
6. Se puede descargar películas y música. Suelo pasar mucho tiempo escuchando música en mi móvil y hace el viaje al colegio mucho más divertido. ¡Qué suerte tenemos! No hay límites.

1. *There is no doubt that mobile phones make communication much easier. The main advantage is that you can communicate with people all over the world*
2. *We can find out about anything whenever we like.*
3. *It helps me with my homework.*
4. *Technology allows me to stay in contact with everyone and I make the most of apps like Whatsapp and Snapchat to communicate with my friends all the time.*
5. *I stay up to date using the news apps which let me know when something important happens*
6. *You can download films and music. I usually spend a lot of time listening to music on my phone and it makes the journey to school much more fun. How lucky we are! There are no limits.*

Disadvantages of technology

1. Lo que más me preocupa es que hoy en día los jóvenes se quedan pegados a sus aparatos y puede ponerse adictos. Pierden la capacidad de comunicar cara a cara y resulta que los estudiantes se vuelven solitarios y tristes.
2. Nos estamos poniendo tan adictos a nuestros aparatos que corremos el riesgo de tener accidentes cuando conducimos o cruzamos la calle.
3. Además, si mandas un mensaje electrónico, esperas una respuesta inmediata y eso puede provocar el estrés y otros problemas de salud.
4. Siempre hay riesgos de virus y la información privada puede ser mal utilizada y corremos el riesgo de ser víctimas de delito informático y del robo de identidad.
5. Otro riesgo del uso de Internet es estar en contacto con desconocidos, especialmente para los jóvenes. Personas peligrosas pueden esconderse detrás de identidades falsas para

que no sepamos quién nos habla en realidad. Por ejemplo, ayer vi las noticias y hablaron sobre una chica de dieciséis años que conoció a su 'novio' a través Facebook, pero en realidad era un hombre viejo y que la mató. ¡Qué chocante!

1. *What worries me most is that nowadays, young people stay glued to their devices and you can become addicted. They lose the capacity to communicate face to face and the result is that students become lonely and sad.*
2. *We are getting so addicted to our devices that we risk having accidents when we are driving or crossing the road.*
3. *In addition, if you send a message electronically, you expect an immediate answer so that pressure can cause stress and other health problems.*
4. *There are always risks of viruses infecting our computers and private information can be misused and we risk being victims of cybercrime and identity theft.*
5. *Another risk of Internet use is being in contact with strangers, especially for young people. Dangerous people can hide behind false identities so that we don't know who we are really speaking too. For example, yesterday I saw the news and they spoke about a 16 year old girl who met her 'boyfriend' on Facebook, but in reality he was an old man who killed her. How shocking!*

The future of mobile phones

En el futuro, creo que los móviles se volverán más flacos con pantallas más grandes y útiles. Pero pase lo que pase serán más poderosos y deberemos tener cuidado con la información que compartimos por internet porque corremos el riesgo de ser víctimas de delito informático.

In the future, I believe that mobiles with become thinner with bigger screens and more useful. But whatever happens they will be more powerful and we will have to be careful with the information we share on the internet because we risk being victims of cybercrime.

SOCIAL ACTIVITIES, FITNESS AND HEALTH

What do you eat on a normal day?

Cada mañana desayuno cereales porque son una fuente de energía Como un bocadillo y fruta al colegio, pero si tuviera la oportunidad me gustaría comer pescado frito con patatas fritas. Al volver a casa, siempre como chocolate, aunque sea malo para la salud, porque soy adicta y se me hace agua la boca. Ceno carne y verduras, pasta, pollo o pizza. Debería comer menos chocolate y más fruta y verduras para evitar enfermedades cardiacas.

Every morning I eat cereal because it is a source of energy and this helps me when I work. I eat a sandwich and fruit at school but if I had the chance I would like to eat fish and chips. On returning home, I always eat chocolate although it is bad for you, because I am addicted and it makes my mouth water. I eat meat and vegetables, pasta, chicken or pizza for dinner. I should eat less chocolate and more fruit and vegetables in order to avoid heart problems.

General eating habits

Intento comer sano, aunque sea bastante difícil de vez en cuando. Como cinco porciones de frutas y verduras al día, y evito el azúcar. Me cuesta a veces porque me encanta comer chocolate y dulces, pero opino que se puede tomar los alimentos no saludables en moderación. Cuando era joven odiaba la comida sana y cada día pedía la comida rápida.

I try to eat healthily although it is quite difficult sometimes. I eat 5 portions of fruit and vegetables per day and I avoid sugar. It's hard sometimes because I love eating chocolate and sweet things but I think it's okay to have unhealthy things in moderation. When I was young I used to hate healthy food and every day I asked for fast food.

What don't you like eating

Suelo comer todo, pero si tuviera elegir un tipo de comida que no me gusta mucho, sería el espárrago.

I usually eat everything, but if I had to choose a type of food that I don't like very much, it would be asparagus.

Lunch at school

Almuerzo en la cantina donde suelo tomar un bocadillo de pollo o una ensalada. Afortunadamente la comida escolar ha mejorado a lo largo de los años, tanto en cuanto a sabor como a nutrición. ¡Qué suerte tenemos! Ayer comí pasta con champiñones. Fue delicioso.

I eat lunch in the canteen where I usually have a chicken sandwich or a salad. Fortunately, school lunches have improved throughout the years, in flavour and in nutrition. How lucky we are!

Favourite food

Mi comida favorita es el chocolate, aunque sea malo para la salud, porque es delicioso y se me hace agua la boca. Como chocolate todos los días, después del colegio para que tenga la energía que necesito para hacer mis deberes.

My favourite food is chocolate although it is bad for my health because it is delicious and makes my mouth water. I eat chocolate every day after school so that I have the energy I need to do my homework.

How to stay healthy

Para llevar una vida sana se debe comer una dieta variada con cinco porciones de fruta o verduras al día, ya que nos dan vitaminas importantes. Deberíamos evitar la comida basura porque contiene demasiado azúcar y grasa y provoca la obesidad. Además, es muy importante que hagamos deporte, evitemos el alcohol y no fumemos, porque puede causar enfermedades graves. Sin embargo, opino que se puede tomar los alimentos no saludables en moderación.

In order to lead a healthy life, we must eat a varied diet with five portions of fruit and vegetables a day because they give us important vitamins. We should avoid junk food because it contains too much sugar and fat and causes obesity. In addition, it's very important to do sport, avoid alcohol and not smoke because it can cause serious illnesses. However, I think that you can eat unhealthy food in moderation.

How you stay healthy

Para mantener la forma hago deporte por lo menos tres veces a la semana al aire libre, bebo dos litros de agua al día y tomo cinco porciones de fruta o verduras. Nunca fumo y nunca he probado una droga. Siempre intento evitar la comida basura y materia grasa, aunque sea difícil porque no puedo prescindir del chocolate, e intento dormir ocho horas como mínimo cada noche.

In order to keep in shape, I do sport at least three times a week in the fresh air, I drink two litres of water a day and I have 5 portions of fruit or vegetables. I never smoke and I have never taken drugs. I always try to avoid junk and fatty foods, although it is difficult because I can't manage without chocolate, and I try to sleep eight hours minimum every night.

Do you like sport?

Sí, me gusta muchísimo el deporte. Es mi asignatura favorita en el colegio porque es fácil y el profesor es divertido. Lo que más me gusta es estar al aire libre. Después de una hora de tenis me siento muy relajado. Suelo jugar al tenis tres veces a la semana, y los sábados me encanta aprovechar el buen tiempo y hacer ciclismo con mi padre. Cuando sea mayor, voy a seguir haciendo deporte para mantener la forma y un buen estado de ánimo.

Yes, I like sport a lot. It is my favourite subject at school because it is easy and the teacher is fun. What I like the most is being in the fresh air. After an hour of tennis I feel very relaxed. I usually play tennis three times a week and on Saturdays I love to make the most of the good weather and go cycling with my father. When I grow up I'm going to carry on doing sport to keep fit and stay happy.

Why should we do sport?

Deberíamos hacer deporte ya que es genial para mejorar el estado de ánimo, reducir el estrés y mantenerse en forma. Se puede también hacer nuevos amigos y aumentar la autoconfianza. Si no hiciéramos deporte, correríamos el riesgo de engordar, y la obesidad puede provocar enfermedades graves.

We should do sport because it is a great way to improve the mood, reduce stress and keep fit. You can also make new friends and improve your self-confidence. If we didn't do sport, we would risk getting fat and obesity can cause serious illnesses.

Todays' health problems

Hay un montón de problemas de salud en mi país, pero lo que más me preocupa es la obesidad. Se dice que casi la mitad de los niños británicos son obesos. Pasan demasiado tiempo delante de la televisión o pegados a sus móviles y no hacen ejercicio. También suelen comer la comida basura porque es barata, sabrosa y fácil a obtener. Contiene mucha grasa, sal y azúcar y eso puede provocar enfermedades como la cardiopatía.

There are loads of health problems in my country. What worries me most is obesity. It is said that almost half of British children are obese. They spend too much time in front of the television or glued to their mobiles and don't exercise. Also they eat junk food because it is cheap, tasty and easy to get. It contains lots of fat, salt and sugar and this can cause illness like heart disease.

The solution to health problems

Es imprescindible que hagamos algo para mejorar la situación. Si fuera ministro de deporte, lanzaría una campaña para enseñar a los niños sobre los beneficios del deporte. Sería genial si hubiera unas personas famosas a las que los jóvenes admiran que podrían motivarles a cambiar su estilo de vida. También, es esencial que haya polideportivos en todos partes para que los jóvenes puedan acceder al deporte fácilmente. Ya existen, pero tienes que ser miembro y es caro, así que los jóvenes no pueden permitírselo.

Además, la comida sana debería ser más barata.

We must do something to improve the situation. If I were minister of sport I would launch a campaign to teach children about the benefits of sport. It would be great if there were some celebrities who young people admired that could motivate them to change their lifestyle. Also, it is essential that there are sports centres everywhere so that young people can access sport easily. They already exist but you have to be a member and it is expensive, therefore young people can't afford it. In addition, healthy food should be cheaper.

Sickness

Tengo suerte porque estoy casi nunca enferma. Normalmente si no es serio, hay que guardar cama, pero si no se siente mejor después de algunos días, tiene que ir al médico. Se puede evitar enfermedades llevando un estilo de vida sano.

I am lucky because I am almost never sick. Normally, if it is not serious you have to stay in bed but if you do not feel better after a few days, you have to go to the doctor. We can avoid illnesses by living a healthy lifestyle.

Smoking

A mi parecer, fumar es absurdo porque todo el mundo sabe que causa enfermedades graves como el cáncer y la bronquitis crónica. Nunca fumaré. Pienso que los jóvenes de hoy en día fuman por un montón de razones, pero lo más importante es la presión del grupo. Si vas a una fiesta y hay muchas personas que están fumando, hay la tentación de hacer lo mismo para sentirse parte del grupo.

In my opinion, smoking is ridiculous because everyone knows that it causes serious illnesses like cancer and chronic bronchitis. I will never smoke. I think that young people today smoke for loads of reasons, but the most important is peer pressure. If you go to a party and there are lots of people smoking, there is the temptation to do the same to feel part of the group.

Alcohol

A mi parecer, el consumo excesivo de alcohol es absurdo porque todo el mundo sabe que causa enfermedades graves como la cirrosis hepática y el cáncer. Nunca beberé de manera excesiva. Pienso que los jóvenes de hoy en día beben alcohol por un montón de razones, pero lo más importante es la presión del grupo. Les falta la autoconfianza y recurren al alcohol para sentirse más valientes. Si vas a una fiesta y hay muchas personas que están borrachas, hay la tentación de hacer lo mismo.

In my opinion, the excessive consumption of alcohol is ridiculous because everyone knows that it causes serious illnesses like cirrhosis of the liver and cancer. I will never drink excessively. I think that young people today drink alcohol for loads of reasons, but the most important is peer pressure. They lack self-confidence and turn to alcohol to feel braver. If you go to a party and there are lots of drunk people, there is the temptation to do the same.

Drugs

A mi parecer, tomar drogas es absurdo porque todo el mundo sabe que causan enfermedades graves como ataques de pánico y pueden alterar la manera cómo funciona el cerebro. Nunca tomaré drogas. Pienso que los jóvenes de hoy en día toman drogas por un montón de razones, pero lo más importante es la presión del grupo. Les falta la autoconfianza y recurren a las drogas para sentirse más valientes. Si vas a una fiesta y hay muchas personas que están tomando drogas, hay la tentación de hacer lo mismo para sentirse parte del grupo.

In my opinion, taking drugs is ridiculous because everyone knows that they cause serious illnesses like panic attacks and can alter brain function. I will never take drugs. I think that young people today take drugs for loads of reasons, but the most important is peer pressure. They lack self-confidence and turn to drugs to feel braver. If you go to a party and there are lots of people taking drugs, there is the temptation to do the same.

Vegetarianism

Hay un montón de razones por el vegetarianismo. No solo es que no quieren matar a los animales sino también tienen razones relacionadas con la salud y el medioambiente. Algunos dicen que comer carne en exceso es malo para la salud y además la producción de carne destruye las selvas tropicales y el medioambiente.

There are many reasons for vegetarianism. Not only do they not want to kill animals but also they have reasons in relation to health and the environment. Some say that eating meat excessively is bad for your health and in addition the production of meat destroys tropical forests and the environment.

Hobbies when you were young

Cuando era joven hacía un poco menos deporte, pero pasaba la mayoría del tiempo en el parque cerca de mi casa, jugando con mis amigos, así que mantenía la forma sin esforzarme. También, veía la tele todos los días y jugaba los videojuegos. Solía leer mucho también.

When I was young I did slightly less sport but I spent the majority of my time in the park near my house, playing with friends so I kept in shape without making an effort. Also, I watched the television every day and played videogames. I used to read a lot as well.

Ideal weekend

Mi fin de semana ideal sería con mi familia y mis amigos. Si pudiera elegir, iría a Londres para ver un espectáculo con mi madre y al volver a mi casa comeríamos pizza. Si fuera posible pasaríamos el día siguiente haciendo natación y jugando a las cartas. ¡Que relajante!

My ideal weekend would be with my family and my friends. If I could choose, I would go to London to watch a show with my mum and on returning home we would eat pizza. If it was possible we would spend the following day swimming and playing cards. How relaxing!

Books you've read

Cuando termino mis deberes, siempre tengo ganas de leer, porque me ayuda a descansar. Sin duda, mi libro favorito es "Harry Potter and the Philosopher's Stone", que acabo de leer por segunda vez. Trata de la escuela Hogwarts de Magia y Hechicería donde Harry conoce a otros niños que tienen poderes especiales y aprende todo lo necesario para ser mago. Para mí lo más importante de leer es poder escaparse del estrés de la vida real.

When I finish my homework, I always want to read because it helps me to relax. Without a doubt my favourite book is "Harry Potter and the Philosopher's Stone" which I have just read for the second time. It is about Hogwarts school of Witchcraft and Wizardry where Harry gets to know other children who have special powers and learns everything necessary to be a wizard. For me the important thing about reading is to escape the stress of real life.

Music and musicians

No toco un instrumento, pero me apasiona la música. Primero me chifla la música electrónica porque es animada y energética. Cuando voy al gimnasio, la escucho para que pueda correr más rápidamente. También la música me ayuda a descansar, por ejemplo, después de un día estresante al colegio lo que más me gusta es escuchar mi artista favorito, Ed Sheeran. Tengo ganas de verlo en concierto, pero las entradas cuestan un ojo de la cara, y primero tengo que hacer mis quehaceres para que pueda permitírmelo.

I do not play an instrument but I love music. Firstly, I like electronic music because it's animated and energetic. What I go to the gym I listen to it so that I can run faster. Also music helps me to relax, for example after a stressful day at school what I like the most is to listen to favourite artist, Ed Sheeran. I want to see him live but first I have to do my chores so that I can afford it.

Pocket money and shopping

Tengo suerte porque mis padres me dan treinta libras al mes. Normalmente suelo comprar revistas y caramelos, pero el fin de semana pasado lo gasté en ir al cine con mis amigos. Si tuviera la oportunidad, me gustaría recibir más dinero para que pudiera comprar más videojuegos, pero mis padres creen que recibo suficiente dinero. ¡Qué pesadilla! No creo que tengan razón.

I am lucky because my parents give me thirty pounds a month. Normally, I buy magazines or videogames, but last weekend I spent it on going to the cinema with my friends. If I had the chance, I would like more money so that I can buy more sweets but my parents think that I receive enough money. What a nightmare! I don't think they are right.

Role play at GCSE

The role play element does not exist yet in all exam boards but is super-useful as an exercise if you want to feel confident out and about in a French-speaking country, some would say essential! Other exam boards give you a short time to prepare a role play exercise where you will usually play the role of a student going to stay with a family, or a tourist needing some information. Be prepared to talk about something going wrong, like leaving your bag in the restaurant, your wallet in the taxi, missing planes and losing passports.

The best way to prepare for this is to revise set phrases that often arise, so they are grouped below in subject matter.

Initiating a conversation

Disculpe	Excuse me
¿Puedo ayudarle?	Can I help you ?
¡Dígame!	Hello (answering phone)
Hola	Hi / Hey
Buenos días / buenas tardes	Hello (formal)
Llamo porque	I'm calling you because
He reservado una habitación	I have reserved a room

Directions

¿Como llego a la estación?	How do I get to the station?
Sigue todo recto	Go straight on
Hasta el semáforo	Until the lights
Toma	Take
La primera a la derecha	the first road on the right

La segunda a la izquierda	the second left
Gira a la derecha	turn right
Gira a la izquierda	turn left

Lateness and reasons for lateness

Lo siento, llego tarde	Sorry I'm late
Voy a llegar tarde	I'm going to arrive late
Mas tarde que previsto	later than planned
El vuelo fue cancelado	the flight was cancelled
Discutí con	I argued with
Perdí el tren	I missed the train

Losing things

He perdido mi pasaporte	I have lost my passport
He dejado mi bolsa en	I left my bag in….
He olvidado mi monedero	I have forgotten my wallet

Asking questions

¿Dónde está la estación?	Where is the station ?
¿A qué hora sale el tren?	When does the train leave?
¿Qué vamos a hacer?	What are we going to do?
¿Qué te gusta comer?	What do you like eating?
¿Cómo estás?	How are you ?
¿Cómo vas al colegio?	How do you get to school?

¿Cómo es tu casa?	What's your house like?
¿Por qué estas triste?	Why are you sad?
¿Cuánto dinero tienes?	How much money have you got?
¿Cuándo salimos?	When are we going out?

However, if there is no question word involved (so no *how, when, where, who, which, how much, what)* then all you have to do is put the question as a statement with a question mark at the end:

¿Tienes un perro?	You have a dog? Do you have a dog?
¿Hace buen tiempo?	Is the weather good?
¿Hay una mesa?	Is there a table?
¿Te gusta el chocolate?	Do you like chocolate?

Understanding instructions in the role play

Whereas the AQA board role play relates closely to the material in the general conversation, Cambridge IGCSE requires the candidate to understand instructions such as

Saluda	say hello
Dile	tell him / her
Explícale	explain to him / her
Contesta	reply
Dale las gracias	thank him / her
Pídele información	ask for information
Expresa satisfacción	express satisfaction
Pregúntale algo sobre	ask him / her something about
Reacciona con entusiasmo	react with enthusiasm
Muestra sorpresa	show surprise

Impressive phrases

To be used to spice up your writing AS WELL AS your oral!

Make sure you have used:

- **Present** (including irregulars and reflexives) to describe what you normally do
  Voy al cine / Hago mis deberes
  I go to the cinema / I do my homework
  with desde hace – vivo aquí desde hace cinco años
  I have lived here for 5 years

- **Present continuous** to describe what is currently happening
  Estoy leyendo un libro
  I am reading a book

- **Perfect** to describe what you have done
  He visto muchas películas, pero la mejor fue …
  I have seen a lot of films but the best one was …..

- **Preterite** to describe events in the past
  Saqué fotos / Tomé el sol
  I took photos / I sunbathed
  AND irregular preterites to show you know them
  Tuve un accidente / Fui al mercado / Puse la mesa
  I had an accident / I went to the market / laid the table

- **Imperfect** to describe repeated actions in the past

  Vivía en el campo / Solía ver la tele todos los días

  I lived in the countryside / I used to watch TV every day

- **Both types of future** tense

  Voy a ir de vacaciones / Haré mis deberes

I am going to go on holiday / I will do my homework

- **Conditional** to describe what would happen if certain conditions were fulfilled

Me gustaría vivir en el campo / Viviría en una casa

I would like to live in the countryside / I would live in a house

- **Pluperfect** to describe what had happened before the action you are describing

Cuando volvimos, el perro había comido el pastel

When we returned, the dog had eaten the cake

- **Present subjunctive** with specific phrases

¡Ojalá tengamos éxito! *Hopefully we shall succeed*

Trabajo para que pueda ir a una buena universidad

I work so that I can go to a good university

In the future – cuando sea mayor voy a ser profe

When I'm older I'm going to be a teacher

- **Imperfect subjunctive with the conditional**

Si pudiera, cambiaría el uniforme

If I could I would change the uniform

- **Pluperfect subjunctive with the past conditional** (not required, but impressive!)

Si hubiera podido, habria hecho mucho más

If I had been able to, I would have done much more

USE VERBS THAT TAKE GERUNDS

- Voy a **seguir** estudiando
  I'm going to carry on studying

- **Paso** mucho tiempo trabajando
  I spend a lot of time working

- La situación **va** empeorando
  The situation is getting worse

- **Voy** al colegio andando
  I walk to school

OTHER VERB STRUCTURES

Después de / antes de comer	before / after eating
Estoy a punto de comer	I am about to eat
Acabo de hacer	have just eaten
Al llegar	on arriving

OPINIONS

Pienso que / Creo que / En mi opinión ......porque

Positive opinions

Vale la pena	it's worth it
Me pone feliz	it makes me happy
Me hace reir	it makes me laugh
Tengo ganas de ir de vacaciones	I feel like
Espero con ganas	I'm looking forward to
Tengo suerte	I am lucky

Lo que más me gusta es que	what I like most is
Tengo buenas notas	I get good marks
Me lo pasé bomba	I had a great time
No puedo prescindir de él	I can't do without it
¡Qué bueno!	How brilliant!
El mejor país del mundo	best country in the world

Negative opinions

Lo que no me gusta es que	what I don't like is that
Lo que más me preocupa es que	what worries me most is that
Estoy harto	I'm sick of it
¡Qué pesadilla!	What a nightmare!
¡Qué horror!	How horrible!

TENGO EXPRESSIONS

Tengo suerte	I'm lucky
Tengo ganas de	I feel like
Tengo frio / calor	I'm cold / hot
Tengo que	I have to
Tengo hambre / sed	I'm hungry / thirsty
Tengo quince años	I'm 15
Tengo razón	I'm right
Tengo miedo	I am afraid
Tengo prisa	I'm in a hurry

COMPARATIVES AND SUPERLATIVES

Más grande que él	bigger than him
Menos divertido que ella	less fun than her
El mejor del mundo	the best in the world
Es tan deportista como yo	he is as sporty as me

DESDE HACE and HACE

Vivo aquí desde hace cinco años	I have been living here 5 years
Hace dos años fui a España	Two years ago I went to Spain

PRECEDING DIRECT AND INDIRECT OBJECT PRONOUNS

Los profes nos dan	The teachers give us
Les encanta la música	I love music
Le regalé un libro	I gave him a book
No me importa	It doesn't matter to me
Lo hago yo	I do it

SUBJUNCTIVE EXPRESSIONS

Si tuviera mucho dinero	If I had a lot of money
Si fuera rico	If I was rich
Si hubiera un cine	If there was a cinema
Si hubiera tenido el tiempo	If I had had the time
Para que pueda	so that I can

Aunque sea	although it is
No pienso que sea	I don't think it is
¡Ojalá pudiera!	If only I could

PARA, SIN + infinitive

Fui al parque para jugar al tenis	I went to the park to play tennis

Los jóvenes toman drogas sin pensar en las consecuencias

Young people take drugs without thinking about the consequences

IMPERSONAL EXPRESSIONS

Se puede	you can (one can)
Se debe / hay que	you must (one must)

PRONOUNS ATTACHED TO THE INFINITIVE / GERUND

No puedo permitírmelo	*I can't afford it*
Para que pueda aprovecharlo	*So I can make the most of it*
Me gustaría verlo en concierto	*I would like to see him in concert*

MODALS IN ALL TENSES

No puedo prescindir de mi móvil	*I can't do without my mobile*
Deberíamos ahorrar agua	We should save water
Podría hacer más ejercicio	I could do more exercise
Solía ver la tele	I used to watch TV
Me gustaría aprender el español	I 'd like to learn Spanish

SPANISH IDIOMS

Siempre está aprovechando de mi

He is always taking advantage of me

He currado un montón esta semana

I've worked really hard this week!

Voy a pegarme un madrugón

I'm going to get up really early

Él es muy madrugador

He's a really early riser

Estoy un poco fastidiado

I'm not feeling very well

Tengo el pie fastidiado	I've hurt my foot
¡Estoy machacado / agotado!	I'm exhausted!
Llueve a mares	It's pouring with rain
Cuesta un ojo de la cara	It costs an arm and a leg
Se me hace agua la boca	It makes my mouth wáter
Tiene un humor de perros	She is in a bad mood
Gastarse un riñon	to pay through the nose
Harina de otro costal	another thing entirely
Domrir como un tronco	to sleep like a log

PART 3

Writing

Your oral answers will be your first port of call when approaching the writing task. But don't churn them out verbatim – check carefully what the question is asking for first. When approaching the long piece of writing, you should base it on what you know well. Don't use any language you haven't used or practised before unless you absolutely have to.

This is your moment!

Like the oral, the writing part of the exam is where you are in charge. You can get top marks here and risk losing a few in the harder parts of the listening. Make this work to your advantage. Where the writing exam really helps is in giving you time to consider your answer, check it and amend it, which you don't get to do in the oral.

Use your oral answers

There are plenty of parallels between the oral and the writing exams. This means that once you are familiar with the oral you will be able to use a lot of the material in the writing. My YouTube channel shows you how to remember the standard answers relating to describing a person, place or activity, and gives you the standard technique to answer questions on technology and environment. So when you're learning the oral answers, just remember you're killing two birds with one stone.

Read the question!

Plenty of people get caught out by questions which *appear* to be one of the standard answers but which only require a section of it. For example, part of the question may require you to talk about the advantages OR disadvantages of the internet, so you're wasting your time doing both. The examiner will think you don't know the meaning of the word *or*. If they ask you specifically what you do at home to help protect the environment, don't talk about public transport because that happens away from the house. If they want you to explain the importance of eating healthily, focus on that rather than on the activities side of the health topic. Where you do venture into other areas, keep them linked clearly to the question you are answering.

Choose your question carefully

Don't plump for the question that appears to be on a topic you know well. First you need to check and double check that you understand what each point is that you need to address. You may be an expert on describing your town by now, but is that what they want, or does the question contain vocabulary that you don't know. Even if there is one word in one bullet point that you don't understand, this could lose you 25% of your available marks.

Leave a line

If you write out the bare bones of your answer using alternate lines, there will be room to go back and fill in the gaps when you remember some key expressions you should have used. This may look a bit odd, but much easier to space it out than to have the examiner struggle to navigate asterisks and tiny handwriting squashed into the gaps.

Check, check and check again

Check that subject and verb agree, and that article, noun and adjective agree. In English we can say I like big houses without bothering with any of that. In Spanish you will need to agree every word *me gustan las casas grandes*.

Do not attempt to express anything you haven't said before

This is not the time or the place to try out new stuff. Stick to what you know. If you're not sure if it's por or para, go another route.

Use my mnemonic

As part of this checking procedure, use this mnemonic, which takes you from L to V in the alphabet. I have listed the letters on the next page, what they stand for, and examples of each.

The writing mnemonic...

Leave a line so you can add things later to increase word count.

Modals

The verbs to have to, to be able to, to want to are all modal verbs and you need to show the examiner that you can use them in all tenses

Tuve que volver a casa	I had to
Deberiamos proteger el medioambiente	We should protect
Se puede hacer deporte	One can do
Quiero ser abogado	I want to be

Negatives

No tengo animales	I don't have
No me gusta el queso	I don't like
Nunca voy al cine	I never go

Opinions

En mi opinión	In my opinión
Creo que	I believe
Pienso que	I think
Me parece que	It seems to me that

Pronouns

Los profes nos dan	The teachers give us
Me levanto	I get up
Lo encuentro fácil	I find it

Qué

¡Qué desastre!	What a disaster!
¡Qué pena!	What a pain!
¡Qué suerte!	How lucky!
¡Qué delicioso!	How delicious!
¡Qué pesadilla!	What a nightmare!

Reasons

Porque, puesto que, dado que	because

Superlatives (and comparatives)

El mejor colegio de Londres	The best school in London
Es más deportista que yo	S/he is more sporty than me

Time phrases

Antes de + infinitive	before (doing something)
Después de + infinitive	After (doing something)
Al llegar	On arriving
Acabo de	I have just
Está a punto de	S/he is about to
Dos veces a la semana	Twice a week
A las cinco de la tarde	At five o'clock in the afternoon
Todos los días	Every day
Bastante a menudo	Quite often

Umbrella (weather!)

Hizo sol	It was hot
Llueve / nieva	It is raining / snowing
Llovía / nevaba	It was raining / snowing
Llovió / nevó	It rained / snowed
Hacía buen tiempo	The weather was good

Verbs

Use all the tenses you can possibly cram in:

Present	eg. hago mucho deporte
Preterite	eg. hizo sol
Imperfect	eg. cuando era pequeño
Perfect	eg. he visitado muchos países
Near Future	eg. voy a ir al cine
Future simple	eg. iremos al teatro
Past subjunctive	eg. si fuera rico
Conditional	eg. compraría una casa
Present subjunctive	eg. es importante que haga sol

PART 4

Reading

Vocabulary

The key to getting a high mark in the reading and the listening is vocabulary. There are vocab lists by topic at the back of this book and you should know all of it by exam day. Yes, all of it.

Word tricks

If you spot a word you recognize, don't jump to conclusions and assume it's the answer to the question you're looking at. Chances are, it's a red herring, so look at the sentence as a whole for meaning and to check there isn't a negative hiding in there which would make the meaning entirely the opposite of what you thought. Remember that *pocos amigos* means *few friends* as opposed to *a few friends* and *sin* means *without*.

Gapfill expectations

When you're doing a gapfill exercise, look carefully at the sentence and work out what kind of word you expect to fill the gap with. If the gap is preceded by an article, it is likely to be a noun, if a noun, it's likely to be an adjective because adjectives generally come after nouns, but expect in each case for there to be at least a couple of options in the box to choose from. If the options are the same adjective but with different endings, look for clues as to the gender of the word it is describing.

Comprehension

Make sure you spend plenty of time on this exercise. You will need to understand the passage, then the question, then be able to locate the part of the passage where the answer is located and make whatever adjustments are required to make that information fit. Often, this is a case of changing something from the first to the third person.

Literary texts

Some questions will be based on original literary texts. It will look impossible, but you can do it with some good detective work. Take your time and use what you know.

Understanding the text of a comprehension passage

Get a basic grasp of it

To start with, read the text twice to get a general idea of what it is about. Focus on what you understand rather than what you don't. If there are words you don't know, use your knowledge of grammar, think whether you can find an English cognate to help, and look at the context, which usually gives a clue to meaning.

Don't sweat the reflexives

Spanish is full of reflexive verbs. This means you will see lots of *se* being used in a reading text. Whenever something *is being done* then in Spanish the reflexive form may be used. Look at this passage from a recent paper:

se tiran fuegos artificiales, se montan conciertos y bailes, se pasea y se come y se bebe en la calle

So you can gather from this that drinks are being drunk and food is being eaten. It doesn't matter what *se tiran* or *se montan* mean, just focus on the fireworks and concerts.

Cognates

There are lots of words in Spanish that you can guess easily because they are so similar to the English.

Words ending in -ic or -ical in English are usually -ico in Spanish

académico, artístico, económico, automático, básico, democrático, clásico, exótico, fantástico, heroico, irónico, mágico, orgánico, plástico, público, romántico, político, psicológico, biológico, físico, cómico

You can also add an o to words ending in ct in English

adicto, conflicto, contacto, correcto, exacto, insecto, perfecto, producto

English words ending in -ous tend to end in -oso in Spanish

religioso, curioso, delicioso, misterioso, tedioso, numeroso, varioso

SO what do these mean?

Un animal brutal

Un error universal

Un club local

Un criminal psicológico

Una pizza deliciosa

Una publicación legal

Un problema global

Un hospital básico

Places in town that you'll recognise

el parque	park
el colegio	school
el supermercado	supermarket
el mercado	market
el centro comercial	shopping centre
el hotel	hotel
el teatro	theatre
el cine	cinema

Words that make sense when you take off the e at the front

estómago	stomach
espinaca	spinach
estudiantes	students

estación	station
estable	stable
estadio	stadium
escándalo	scandal
escenario	scandal
Escocia	Scotland
escuela	school
espacio	space
España	Spain
especial	special
espectador	spectator
espinal	spinal
esposo	spouse / husband
esposa	spouse / wife
esquí	skiing
estatua	statue
estrés	stress
estricto	strict
estupendo	amazing (stupendous)

Spanish words that have cognates in French

biblioteca	library
fácil	easy
difícil	difficult
malo	bad
mal	badly
bicicleta	bike
jardín	garden
grande	big
enorme	enormous
tranquilo	quiet
simpático	nice
avión	plane
pan	bread
té	tea
fresas	strawberries
frambuesas	raspberries
viejo	old
bien	well
aprender	to learn
el mar	sea
fumar	to smoke
profesor	teacher

Questions used in comprehensions

Cuándo – here, look out for the use of *desde hace* which expresses how long something has been going on, and *hace* meaning *ago,* both of which may trip you up.

Vive allí desde hace dos años - she has lived there for 2 years

Llegó hace dos años – she arrived 2 years ago

Por qué – if the question asks why, you may answer using *porque* = *because* and make sure you also answer the question in the right tense and using the right person. So, if the narrator says *fui a la tienda porque tuve que comprar pan,* your answer can be lifted from the passage except for *fui* which changes to *fue* and *tuve (I had to)* which must change to *tuvo (he / she had to)*

Cómo es – the word *cómo* literally means *how* but when followed by the verb *ser* in any form, it will be asking what something or someone is like. So *Cómo es su casa?* means *What is his/herhouse like?*

Cómo sabemos que – *how do we know that…* needs to be answered with a piece of evidence, and you may be asked for two pieces of evidence, so if there are two marks, make sure you have two answers.

Cuál es / Qué es – both of these mean *what is* and may be seen in the plural form *cuales / que son* meaning *what are.*

Explica…. – you may have to explain something, which means turning it into your own words, so think of a way of explaining it which is clear and simple. Look at the Listening section of this book for ideas on synonyms.

PART 5

Listening

Vocabulary and Synonyms

A key element to doing well in the listening is vocabulary. To have a chance of getting a good mark, you will need to have a good grasp of the word lists set out at the back of this book. However, it is in this part of the exam that you need to be aware of more than one Spanish word for the English – so for example, there are at least three words for "job" along with associated adjectives. Good knowledge of synonyms is essential to your success, so I have grouped some of the main words you need below, in categories relating to their meaning. They have been taken from past papers over the last four years or so.

Work and employment

This topic comes up very frequently. It's important that you know and recognise all the different words for work, job, company and pay. Watch out for *poco* because it means *little* but with a negative connotation – as in *not very much.*

Trabajo	work, job
Empleo	job
Carrera	career
Laboral	work (adjective)
Experiencia laboral	work experience
Trabajador	hardworking
Una compañía	company
Una empresa	a company. enterprise
El sueldo	salary
La paga	pay
Ganar dinero	to earn money
Gano poco	I don't earn much
La huelga	strike

School and education

Linked to the topic of employment, you need to be aware of synonyms relating to education. Lots of the words here begin with E…

La escuela	school
El insti(tuto)	school
Escolar	school (adjective)
La comida escolar	school dinners
Estudios	studies, schoolwork
Estudiar	to study
Estudiantes	students
Enseñar	to teach
La enseñanza	education
Lenguas	languages
Los idiomas	languages
Extranjeros	foreign

Necessity

You may need to ascertain whether something is optional, compulsory, possible or prohibited.

Tengo que	I have to
Hay que	it is necessary / one must
Necesito	I need
Deberia	I / S/he, it should
Obligatorio	compulsory
Hace falta	it is necessary

Prohibido	prohibited
Optativo	optional

Health

Don't get salty and salad mixed up and remember that *rico* is a positive food descriptor. *Comida* means lunch as well as food, and *alimento* also means food, which should remind you of the alimentary canal. Check you know the food lists at the back of this book as well.

La salud	health
Saludable	healthy
Sano	healthy
Poco saludable	unhealthy
El ocio	leisure
Actividades	activities
Enfermo	ill
Enfermedad	illness
Enfermero/-a	nurse
Me duele la cabeza	my head hurts
El dolor	pain
El médico	doctor
Mejor	better
Mejorar	to improve
La comida	food OR lunch
Alimentos	food
Comida basura	junk food
Comida rápida	fast food

Alimentos grasos	fatty food
El azúcar	sugar
Azucarado	sweet
Dulce	sweet
Los dulces	sweet things
Caramelos	sweets
Salado /-a	salty
La ensalada	salad
Sabroso	tasty
El sabor	flavour
Delicioso	delicious
Rico	tasty (food) OR rich (money)
Asqueroso	disgusting
Postre	pudding

Ll words

English students famously muddle all the Spanish words beginning with Ll. Here are the most common ones that tend to confuse:

Llevar	to wear
Llevo un uniforme	I wear a uniform
Llevarse bien	to get on
Nos llevamos bien	we get on well
Llegar	to arrive
La llegada	arrival
Llueve	it's raining

Llovió	it rained
Llovía	it was raining
La lluvia	rain

Prices

I have yet to see a listening exam which doesn't mention the cost of things, so make sure you're aware of all the ways this can appear:

Caro	expensive
Precios altos	high prices
Precios bajos	low prices
Costar	to cost
Cuesta mucho	it costs a lot
De alto coste	expensive
Costoso	costly
Cuesta poco	it doesn't cost much
Barato	cheap
De bajo coste	cheap
Gratis	free

Positive reactions

You will need to know all the different ways of expressing likes and dislikes, and associated phrases which imply liking or disliking:

Me gusta	I like (it)
Me gustan	I like (them)
Le gusta	S/he likes (it)
Le gustan	S/he likes (them)
Les gusta	They like (it)

Les gustan	They like (them)
Me encanta	I love
Cómico	funny
Gracioso	funny
Divertido	fun
Divertirse	to have fun
Disfrutar	to enjoy
Me hace reír	it makes me laugh
Me hace sonreír	it makes me smile
Me hace feliz	it makes me happy
Me hace contento	it makes me happy
Me hace sentir bien	it makes me feel good
Me da energía	it gives me energy
Me dan energía	they give me energy
De mis sueños	of my dreams
Un placer	a pleasure
Pasarlo bien	to have a good time
Pasarlo mal	to have a bad time
Me lo pasé bomba	I had a great time
Mejor	better
Mejorar	to improve

Negative reactions

Difícil / duro	hard
Odio	I hate

Asqueroso	disgusting
Aburrido	boring
Molesto	annoying
Aburrirse	to get bored
Monótono	boring, monotonous
Me cuesta	I find it hard
Lo encuentro duro	I find it hard
Peor / empeorar	worse / to get worse
Decepcionado	disappointed
Me fastidia / molesta	it annoys me

Time and routine

Knowing when and how often someone does something can be critical to getting the answer right.

La rutina	routine
La vida cotidiana	daily life
Todos los días	every day
Todo el día	all day
Siempre	always
A veces	sometimes
de vez en cuando	sometimes, from time to time
Una vez al mes	once a month
Dos veces a la semana	twice a week
Muchas veces	often
A menudo	often

Nunca	never
Suelo salir	I usually go out
Con retraso	delayed
Tarde	late
Temprano	early

Walking

Ir a pie	to go on foot
Ir andando	to walk
Andar	to walk
Caminar	to walk
Dar un paseo	to go for a walk
Dar una vuelta	to go for a walk / ride

The *que* sound

This sounds like *kay* and is not only a word on its own meaning either what, which or than, but the first syllable of a few commonly misunderstood words:

Quedarse	to stay / remain
Me quedo	I stay
Me quedé	I stayed
Quejarse	to complain
Se quejan	they complain
Quemar	to burn
Quemado	burnt
Querer	to want / love
Querido	dear, loved

Queso	cheese

Something and nothing, up and down, success and failure

Here are a few words that can drastically change the meaning of a sentence:

Algo	something
Algunos casos	some cases
Nunca	never
Nada	nothing
Ningún	no
Tampoco	neither
Nadie	nobody
Cualquier	any
Aumentar	to go up, increase
El aumento	the increase
Subir	to go up
Tener éxito	to succeed
Diminuir	to go down
Bajar	to lower, get out of
Ha bajado	it has gone down
Suspender	to fail
Sacar un reprobado	to fail

Starting and stopping

Empezar	to begin
Comenzar	to begin, commence

Al principio	at the beginning
Parar	to stop
Pararse	to stop (oneself0
El autobús se paró	the bus stopped
Acabar	to stop or to have just
Acabo de llegar	I have jut arrived
Dejar de fumar	to stop smoking

Past participles

He dicho (from decir)	I have said
Han hecho (from hacer)	They have done
Has vuelto (from volver)	You have returned
Ha visto (from ver)	S/he has seen
Habéis puesto (from poner)	You (pl) have put / laid
Ha muerto (from morir)	S/he has died
Hemos roto (from romper)	We have broken
Ha sido (from ser)	It has been
Un hecho	A fact

Gerunds

Ing in English words usually corresponds to *ando* or *iendo* in Spanish ones, but sometimes where the infinitive is short, as in *ser, ver, ir, dar,* you end up with more ending than verb, which can be disconcerting to the English ear:

Viendo	watching
Dando	giving
Yendo	going

Siendo	being
Va empeorando	it's getting worse
Va mejorando	it's getting better
Seguir estudiando	to carry on studying

Preterites

As with the gerunds above, some preterite forms bear little resemblance to the original infinitive:

Hice	I did / made
Hizo	S/he did / made
Hizo sol	it was sunny
Hicieron	they did / made
Puse	I put (past)
Puso	S/he put
Pusieron	They put
Tuve	I had
Tuvo	S/he had
Hubo	There was (occurred)
Pude	I was able to
Pudo	S/he was able to
Pudieron	They were able to
Fui	I went
Fue	S/he went / was
Fueron	They were / went

Dije	I said / told
Dijo	S/he said / told
Di	I gave
Dio	S/he gave
Dieron	They gave
Estuve	I was (in a place)
Estuvo	S/he was (in a place)
Estuvieron	They were (in a place)
Vine	I came
Vino	S/he came
Vinieron	They came

P words

Pelirojo	red-haired
Peligroso	dangerous
Película	film
Peluquero	hairdresser
Peluquería	hairdresser's shop
Pelearse	to fight
Perezoso	lazy

Numbers

Trece	13
Treinta	30
Cincuenta	50
Quinientos	500

Cinco	5
Quince	15
Catorce	14
Cuatro	4
Cuarenta	40

Heat

El calor	heat
Caliente	hot
El calentamiento global	global warming
La calefacción	heating
Caloroso	warm

Tener expressions

Tener éxito	to succeed
Tener hambre	to be hungry
Tener sed	to be thirsty
Tener miedo	to be afraid
Tener razón	to be right
Tener cuenta	to take account
Tener lugar	to take place
Tener calor	to be hot

Top tips for the listening

Do as many papers as you can and learn vocabulary!

Each exam board has a slightly different question style. Using the exam board website, do as many past papers as possible and check your answers using the mark scheme. Students who know the most vocab get the highest marks.

Use the reading time

Use every second of the preparation time you are given, to assess what you need to be listening out for. In the more complex comprehension passages, it is a good idea to know what to listen out for before the passage starts playing and will make the listening task less stressful.

Don't write and listen at the same time

Believe it or not, actual multitasking is pretty much impossible. Girls and women tend to be better at switching between tasks quickly, but don't rely on writing your answers at the same time as listening to the audio. Imagine you're listening to a friend talking – you don't need to write everything down then do you? Think of this exercise as similar to that. If you have read the questions and can develop a code for notes (see below) then the rest of the work is just building a picture in your mind of what is being said, just as you would do when listening to a friend.

Practise writing notes

Even if you don't manage to do full practice papers, you can listen to the radio, to recordings on exam websites or on BBC Bitesize, and practise making notes using symbols and abbreviations that don't take up valuable time. For example, a big pound / dollar sign might mean expensive, and a small one cheap. You can draw arrows to indicate travel, and numbers are quick to write when it comes to dates, room numbers and ages. After listening to a few tracks from previous papers you will see how the same themes recur and you can develop your own code system to represent the words you hear.

Look out for negatives and superlatives

They will be trying to trip you up, you can bet on it. Watch out for words like *nunca, tampoco, nadie, ningun,* which will change the meaning of the sentence entirely. Similarly, someone might talk about what they like using *me gusta* but if they end up saying *prefiero (I prefer)* or *sobre todo (most of all)* then that is the thing they like most and that will be your answer.

You don't need to understand every word

There is always going to be the odd word you don't know. Don't panic. Part of the exercise is using your initiative to work out what words and phrases mean from the context you find them in. For example, you might hear this:

Los documentales pueden ser una herramienta educativa

What does herramienta mean? Well, the sentence means "documentaries can be an educational *something*"

Does it matter what it means? Probably not, because the thing is, you have the gist here – basically that documentaries are educational.

Herramienta means *tool* by the way, in case you were wondering!

PART 6

Vocabulary lists by topic

RELATIONSHIPS AND DESCRIBING PEOPLE

Family

en mi familia	in my family
mi padre	my father
mi madre	my mother
mis padres	my parents
mis hermanos	my siblings
mi hermano	my brother
mi hermana	my sister
mis hermanastros	my step-siblings
mi hermanastro	my half or step-brother
mi hermanastra	my half or step-sister
mayor / menor	older/younger
soy hijo único	I'm an only child *(unique)*
mis abuelos	my grandparents
mi primo / mi prima	my cousin
mi tío	my uncle *(go for tea oh?)*
mi tía	my aunt
gemelos, gemelas	twins
el hijo	son
la hija	daughter
el bebé	baby
el marido	husband *(married-o)*
la mujer / esposa	wife
el chico	boy
la chica	girl
no tengo hermanos	I don't have any siblings
mi hermano se llama	my brother is called

How you get on

nos llevamos bien	we get on well
tenemos mucho en común	we have a lot in common
nos gusta	we like (a singular thing)
nos gustan	we like (plural things)
nos gusta la misma música	we like the same music
nos gustan los mismos programas	we like the same programmes
a veces discutimos	sometimes we argue
estar mimado	to be spoilt
no le gusta(n)	he / she doesn't like
no le gusta mi música	he / she doesn't like my music

Types of family

hay muchos tipos de familia	there are lots of types of family
familias tradicionales	traditional families
familias monoparentales	single-parent families
familias ensambladas	blended families
personas solteras	single people
el número crece	the number is growing
cada vez más	more and more
tienen su valor	they have their value
buenas relaciones	good relations
una relación	a relationship

enamorarse de alguien	to fall in love with someone
el amor	love
conocer a	to meet
se conocen	they meet
se conocen desde hace	they have known each other for
el novio / la novia	boyfriend / girlfriend
casarse con	to marry *(house yourself)*
estar casado /-a	to be married
están casados	they are married
un vínculo	a bond
prometer	to promise
volver a casarse	to remarry
se volvió a casarse	he / she remarried
se volvieron a casarse	they remarried
una pareja	a couple *(pair)*
embarazada	pregnant
fiel	faithful
leal	loyal
juntos	together *(roads at junction)*
una cita	a date
un beso	a kiss
un abrazo	a hug *(brazo = arm)*
contar con	to rely on *(count on)*
estar divorciado /-a	to be divorced
estar separado /-a	to be separated
una familia monoparental	single parent family
estar preocupado	to be worried
discutir	to argue

discutimos sobre	we argue about
llorar	to cry
echar de menos	to miss
la echo de menos	I miss her
lo importante	the important thing
lo único	the only thing

Example

Hay un montón de tipos de familia hoy en día y todos tienen su valor. El número de personas solteras crece y cada vez más niños viven con hermanastros. Lo importante es el amor y la estabilidad y que un niño pueda contar con su familia para todo.

There are loads of types of family nowadays and they all have their value. The number of single people is growing, and more and more children live with half-sisters and brothers. The important thing is love and stability and that a child can rely on his or her family for everything.

.

Adjectives to describe people

grande	big
pequeño /-a	small *(like a Pekinese dog)*
alto /-a	tall *(altitude)*
bajo /-a	short *(base)*
simpático /-a	nice *(sympathetic)*
antipático /-a	not nice
alegre	cheerful
triste	sad *(in need of treats!)*
hablador /-a	chatty *(from hablar = to speak)*
trabajador /-a	hardworking *(from trabajar = to work)*
terco /-a	stubborn

delgado /-a	thin (*delicate*)
gordo /-a	fat
interesante	interesting
aburrido /-a	boring
divertido-a	fun *(diverting)*
gracioso/-a	funny (*gracias for being funny*)
serio /-a	serious
valiente	brave *(valliant)*
fuerte	strong *(a fort is strong)*
débil	weak *(a debilitating illness)*
cariñoso /-a	kind
amistoso /-a	friendly *(from amigo)*
tacaño /- a	mean
travieso /-a	naughty
pesado /-a	annoying
guapo /-a	good looking
feo /-a	ugly
viejo /-a	old
joven	young
deportista	sporty
perezoso /-a	lazy
orgulloso /-a	proud
comprensivo /-a	understanding
cortés	polite
educado /-a	polite
maleducado /-a	rude
maduro /-a	mature
sensible	sensitive

honorable	honorable
honesto /-a	honest
sincero /-a	sincere

Some lovely cognates for descriptions

activo /-a	active
tímido /-a	shy
modesto /-a	modest
arrogante	arrogant
ambicioso /-a	ambitious
artístico /-a	artistic
agresivo /-a	aggressive
prudente	careful
creativo /-a	creative
convencional	conventional
generoso /-a	generous
desorganizado /-a	disorganized
elegante	smart, elegant
famoso /-a	famous
fascinante	fascinating
atlético /-a	athletic
contento /-a	happy
culpable	guilty
imaginativo /-a	imaginative
impulsivo /-a	impulsive
intolerante	intolerant
optimista	optimistic
pesimista	pessimistic

popular	popular
religioso /-a	religious
reservado /-a	reserved
romántico /-a	romantic
sarcástico /-a	sarcastic
superficial	superficial
sociable	sociable
diplomático /-a	diplomatic
tradicional	traditional
inteligente	clever
estúpido -/a	stupid
extravertido	extrovert

There are more, but this gives you an idea of how many words you know without knowing you know them…

Qualifying your adjectives

siempre	always
a veces	sometimes
a menudo	often
muy	very
extremadamente	extremely
bastante	quite
un poco	a bit
más / menos…. que yo	more / less … than me

Hair adjectives – "tengo el pelo …"

largo	long
corto	short

liso	straight
rizado	curly
rubio	blonde
marrón	brown
castaño	dark brown
negro	black
pelirrojo	red

General appearance

es calvo	he is bald
es bajo	he is short
es alto	he is tall
lleva gafas	he wears glasses
una barba	a beard *(like barbed wire)*
tiene barba	he has a beard
un bigote	a moustache *('e got a' 'bigote')*
tiene bigote	he has a moustache
parezco a mi madre	I look like my mother
parece a su madre	he / she looks like his / her mother
nos parecemos	we look like each other

Example

Mi madre tiene el pelo rubio y los ojos marrones. Es muy inteligente, pero a veces un poco tímida, y menos extravertida que yo. Normalmente nos llevamos bien porque tenemos muchas cosas en común como el deporte, pero a veces discutimos cuando no quiere que salga con mis amigas en vez de hacer mis deberes.

My mother has blonde hair and brown eyes. She is very intelligent but sometimes a bit shy, and less outgoing than I am. Normally we get on well because we have a lot in common like sport, but sometimes we argue because she doesn't want me to go out with my friends instead of doing my homework.

Clothes and things you carry

una camisa	a shirt *(camisole)*
una camiseta	a t-shirt *(litte camisa)*
pantalones	trousers *(pants are long)*
vaqueros	jeans
un vestido	a dress *(long vest)*
una falda	a skirt *('folded' pleats?)*
los guantes	gloves
calcetines	socks *(concertina down legs)*
un cinturón	a belt *(from cintura = waist)*
una corbata	tie *(bat the flies away with it)*
una chaqueta	a jacket
un gorro	woolly hat
gafas	glasses
un paraguas	umbrella *(para agua = for water)*
un jersey	a jumper
zapatos	shoes
zapatillas de deporte	trainers
un abrigo	an overcoat
un impermeable	a raincoat *(impermeable)*
un monedero	wallet *(keep your 'money der')*
una maleta	suitcase *(need a mallet to shut it)*
una bolsa	a bag

un reloj	a watch or clock

Describing clothes

rayado /-a	striped
a cuadros	checked *(quadrants)*
ajustado /-a	tight *(needs adjusting!)*
con puntitos	spotty *(punto = dot)*
de cuero	leather
de lana	woollen *(from a llama?)*
de seda	silk
de algodón	cotton *(coddon)*
la moda	fashion
la marca	the brand

Colours

rojo /-a	red
naranja	orange *(a 'norange')*
amarillo /-a	yellow
azul	blue *(azure)*
marrón	brown
rosa	pink *(like roses)*
gris	grey
blanco /-a	white
negro /-a	black
verde	green *(verdant)*
morado /-a	purple

HOUSE, HOME AND ROUTINE

Houses and flats

una casa	a house
independiente	detached
adosada	semi-detached / terraced
en hilera	terraced
un piso / un apartamento	a flat
en la planta baja	on the ground floor
en el primer piso	on the first floor
en el segundo piso	on the second floor
la puerta principal	the front door
la puerta trasera	the back door

Rooms

la habitación	room *(you inhabit it)*
el dormitorio	bedroom *(dormitory)*
la cocina	kitchen *('cook-in-a' kitchen)*
el jardín	garden
el salón	lounge *(saloon)*
el garaje	garage
el vestíbulo	hall
el descansillo	landing
el comedor	dining room *(from comer=to eat)*
el despacho	office *(send your dispatches)*
la terraza interior	conservatory *(interior terrace)*
el balcón	balcony
un lavadero	utility room
una sala de juegos	games room

Structure

el edificio	building *(Eddy fixed it)*
la ventana	window *(for ventilation)*
la puerta	door *(port is a door to a country)*
las paredes	walls *(a pair of Eddy's)*
el tejado	roof
el techo	ceiling
la escalera	staircase *(escalator)*
la calefacción central	central heating

Furniture

los muebles	furniture
el armario	wardrobe *(for your 'armour')*
la cómoda	chest of drawers
la alfombra	rug
la cama	bed
la almohada	pillow
la estantería	bookshelf *('it stand here')*
el lavaplatos	dishwasher
la lavadora	washing machine
el grifo	tap *(grip it)*
el espejo	mirror *(looking 'especially' lovely)*
el horno	oven
el césped	lawn
el árbol	tree
la hierba	grass *(green herbs)*
las flores	flowers
detrás de	behind *(leave trash behind)*

delante de	in front of *(you leant on it)*
al lado de	next to *('a lad' next to you)*
cerca de	near
compartir	to share *(into compartments)*
limpio	clean *(limp after all the cleaning)*
sucio	dirty
desordenado	untidy
los vecinos	neighbours *('they've seen us!')*

Household jobs

suelo	I usually
suelo pasar la aspiradora	I usually do the hoovering

Think of somone passing the doorway with the "aspirator" machine that breathes in (like respiration) all the dust

poner la mesa	to lay the table
quitar la mesa	to clear the table
lavar los platos	to wash the dishes
preparar la comida	to do the cooking
arreglar mi dormitorio	to tidy my room
ayudar a mis padres	to help my parents
lavar el coche	to wash the car
limpiar la cocina	to clean the kitchen
hacer jardinería	to do the gardening
sacar la basura	to take out the rubbish *(in a sack)*
hacer de canguro	to do babysitting *(with baby in pouch)*
llenar el lavaplatos	to fill the dishwasher

Example

Suelo arreglar mi dormitorio y limpiar la cocina y a veces paso la aspiradora, pero no lo hago todos los días porque los profes nos dan demasiados deberes.

I usually tidy my room and clean the kitchen and sometimes I do the hoovering, but I don't do it every day because the teachers give us too much homework.

Daily routine

Me levanto	I get up
Me ducho	I shower
Me visto	I get dressed
Desayuno	I have breakfast
Tomo un café	I have a coffee
Voy al colegio	I go to school
Llego al colegio	I arrive at school
Juego con mis amigos	I play with my friends
Voy a mis clases	I go to my lessons
Vuelvo a casa	I go home
Hago mis deberes	I do my homework
Ceno	I have dinner
Veo la tele	I watch TV
Me acuesto	I go to bed

HOME AND ABROAD

el país	country
la región	region
el barrio	neighbourhood
la ciudad	city / town
el pueblo	village
en el campo	in the countryside
la mejor región de…	the best region of
en mi barrio	in my area *(barriers protect)*
en la ciudad	in the city *(-dad ending = ity)*
en mi pueblo	in my village
mucho que hacer	a lot to do
vivo aquí desde hace…	I have lived here for…
las ventajas	advantages

Places in the town

hay	there is / are
un lugar / un sitio	place *(lug your stuff there)*
donde se puede	where you can
un cine	cinema
restaurantes	restaurants
polideportivos	sports centres
colegios	schools
un centro comercial	a shopping centre
mercados	markets
supermercados	supermarkets
iglesias	churches
parques	parks

almacenes	department stores
tiendas	shops
fábricas	factories
una playa	a beach
una piscina	a pool
la acera	the pavement
la zona peatonal	the pedestrian zone
la red de transporte	the transport network

Things to do in town

visitar	to visit
museos	museums
un palacio	palace
un castillo	castle
una galería	gallery
un monumento	monument
sitios turísticos	tourist attractions
sitios históricos	historical sites
restaurantes	restaurants
ir al restaurante	to go to the restaurant
comer	to eat
teatros	theatres
ir al teatro	to go to the theatre
ver un espectáculo	to see a show
una obra de teatro	a play
cines	cinemas
ir al cine	to go to the cinema
ver una película	to see a film

ir a la pista de hielo	to go to the ice rink
hacer patinaje	to go skating
ir a la piscina	to go to the pool
hacer natación	to go swimming
nadar	to swim
ir de compras	to go shopping
hacer deporte	to do sport
ir a la bolera	to go bowling
salir por la noche	to go out at night
salir a bailar	to go out dancing
salir a comer	to go out to eat
pasear al perro	to walk the dog
dar paseos	to go for walks
dar una vuelta en bici	to go for a bike ride
montar en bici	to cycle
hacer ciclismo	to cycle
descansar	to rest / relax
encontrarse con amigos	to meet up with friends
tomar una copa	to have a drink
estudiar	to study

Past and future living

cuando era joven	when I was young
vivía en el campo	I lived in the countryside
había menos tiendas	there were fewer shops
era menos ruidoso	it was less noisy
cuando sea mayor	when I'm older
voy a seguir viviendo aquí	I'm going to carry on living here

| para que pueda | so that I can |
| aprovechar | to make the most of |

Town positives

lo bueno es que	the good thing is that
lo que más me gusta es	what I like most is
paso mucho tiempo	I spend lots of time
suelo pasar tiempo	I usually spend time
recomendaría	I would recommend
se puede	one can
no hay que...	it isn't necessary to...
no tienes que...	you don't have to...

Town negatives and improvements

lo malo es que	the bad thing is that
lo que falta es	what's missing is
lo que no me gusta es	what I don't like is
no hay	there isn't a... / there aren't any...
hay que	it is necessary to
tienes que	you have to
no se puede	one can't
desventajas	disadvantages
atascos	traffic jams *('a task' getting through)*
el tráfico	the traffic
la contaminación	the pollution
los coches producen	the cars produce
gases de escape	exhaust fumes
el ruido	the noise *(ruins it all)*

tirar basura	to drop litter
la gente tira basura	people drop litter
caro	expensive *(expensive car)*
la calle	the street
lleno	full
sucio	dirty
concurrido	busy, crowded
si pudiera	if I could
cambiaría	I'd change
construiría	I'd build
mejoraría	I'd improve
me gustaría tener	I'd like to have
aunque sea	although it is
no me gusta(n)	I don't like
me preocupa	it worries me
me fastidia	it annoys me

Shopping

ir de compras	to go shopping
ir a comprar	to go shopping
hacer la(s) compra(s)	to go shopping (for provisions)
comprar	to buy
devolver	to return
ir al centro comercial	to go to the shopping centre
abierto	open *(open 'a-beer-too'!)*
cerrado	closed
dinero	money *('dinner' money)*
el descuento	discount

hacer cola	to queue *(for coca 'cola')*
gastar	to spend *(on 'gas' bill)*
malgastar	to waste *(bad spend)*
demasiado grande	too big
demasiado pequeño	too small
ahorrar	to save
baratas / rebajas	sales
el vendedor (-a)	shop assistant
probarse	to try on
una tarjeta de crédito	a credit card
no puedo permitírmelo	I can't afford it
mirar escaparates	to go window-shopping

Countryside

mudarse	to move house
en el campo	in the countryside
hay menos ruido	there is less noise
es menos concurrido	it's less crowded
tranquilo	quiet
bonito	pretty
el paisaje	the scenery
vacío	empty *(vacant)*
espacios verdes	green spaces
aislado	isolated
difícil desplazarse	difficult to get about
al aire libre	in the fresh air

Example

Cuando sea mayor voy a seguir viviendo en la ciudad porque hay muchas cosas que hacer y para que pueda aprovechar la red de transporte. En el campo, aunque sea bonito, es demasiado tranquilo y aburrido.

When I'm older I'm going to carry on living in the city because there is a lot to do and so that I can make the most of the transport network. In the countryside, although it's pretty, it's too quiet and boring.

Transport

el transporte público	public transport
en autobús	by bus
en tren	by train
en coche	by car
en barco	by boat
en bici	by bike
en avión	by plane *(aviation)*
la estación de trenes	the train station
tomar el tren	to take the train
en el andén	on the platform
comprar billetes	to buy tickets
un billete de ida y vuelta	return ticket
la taquilla	ticket office
la consigna	left luggage office
subir al tren	to get on the train
subir al taxi	to get in the taxi
bajar del tren	to get off the train
bajar del taxi	to get out of the taxi
perdí el tren	I missed the train

a pie	on foot
voy andando	I walk
caro	expensive *(expensive car)*
barato	cheap *(cheap bar)*
la parada de autobuses	the bus stop
rutas para ciclistas	cycle paths
una red de transporte	a transport network
tardo una hora en ir al…	it takes me an hour to get to…

Example

En mi barrio la red de transporte es estupenda. Se puede viajar en tren, en autobús y en metro. Suelo ir al colegio en coche, pero si hubiera más rutas para ciclistas iría en bici. Ayer, fui a la estación de trenes para comprar billetes de ida y vuelta a Madrid. Fui corriendo al andén, pero perdí el tren. ¡Qué lástima!

In my neighbourhood the transport network is amazing. You can travel by train, bus and underground. I usually go to school by car but if there were more cycle paths I would go by bike. Yesterday I went to the train station to buy return tickets to Madrid. I ran to the platform but I missed the train. What a shame!

Holidays

ir de vacaciones	to go on holiday
el año pasado	last year
el año próximo	next year
hace cinco años	5 years ago
reservar	reserve
una habitación	a room
un hotel	a hotel

Getting there

fui a …. con ….	I went to…. with…..
pasé dos semanas	I spent two weeks
durante dos semanas	for two weeks
el vuelo	the flight
el viaje	the journey *(voyage)*
en el extranjero	abroad *(strangers)*
durar	to last
el vuelo duró	the flight lasted
hacer las maletas	to pack the suitcases
deshacer las maletas	to unpack the suitcases
el equipaje	the luggage
seguro /-a	sure, safe
la seguridad	security *(-dad ending = ity)*

Accommodation

alojarse	to stay *(lodge yourself)*
el alojamiento	accommodation
un apartamento	a flat
un albergue	a hostel
un camping	a campsite
el hotel estaba	the hotel was situated
cerca de la playa	near the beach
la arena	the sand *(from sandy arenas)*
la entrada	entrance
la salida	exit / departure
los servicios / aseos	toilets
la vista	view

llegar	to arrive *(on your legs)*
había	there were / there was

Things to do on holiday

se puede	one can
probar actividades nuevas	try new activities
sacar fotos	to take photos
probar los platos típicos	the local food
tomar el sol	to sunbathe
enviar cartas postales	to send postcards
comprar recuerdos	to buy souvenirs *(a record)*
relajarse / descansar	to relax
divertirse	to have fun
conocer a gente nueva	to meet new people
salir a bailar	to go out dancing

Holiday positives

me lo pasé bomba	I had a great time
tengo ganas de	I would like to
volver	to go back
en el futuro	in the future
esperar	to hope / wait for
esperar con ganas	to look forward to
lo bueno fue que	the good thing was that
hizo sol	it was sunny
lo mejor fue	the best thing was
inolvidable	unforgettable

Holiday negatives

lo malo fue que	the bad thing was that
hizo frio	it was cold
perdí mi pasaporte	I lost my passport
olvidé los billetes	I forgot the tickets
perdió su móvil	he / she lost his / her mobile
me di cuenta	I realised
había perdido	I had lost
había dejado mi móvil	I had left my mobile
perdí el avión	I missed the plane *(lost it)*
el retraso	the delay
lo peor	the worst thing
tuve un accidente	I had an accident
tuve que ir al hospital	I had to go to hospital

Weather

hace sol	it's sunny
hace calor	it's hot
hace frio	it's cold
hace viento	it's windy
llueve	it's raining
hay tormentas	it is stormy
hay niebla	it's foggy
nieva	it's snowing
la lluvia	rain
las nubes	clouds
el cielo	the sky

Example

El año pasado fui a España en avión con mi familia. Nos alojamos en un hotel cerca del mar durante dos semanas. Nadé en el mar, jugué al tenis y visité sitios turísticos. Me lo pasé bomba. Sin embargo, el ultimo día al llegar al aeropuerto me di cuenta de que había perdido mi pasaporte y tuve que volver al hotel. ¡Que desastre!

Last year I went to Spain by plane with my family. We stayed in a hotel near the sea for two weeks. I swam in the sea, played tennis and visited tourist attractions. I had a great time. However, on the last day on arriving at the airport I realised I had lost my passport and I had to go back to the hotel. What a disaster!

Festivals

las fiestas	festivals
el Año Nuevo	New Year
la Navidad	Christmas
el árbol de Navidad	Christmas tree
la boda	wedding
el nacimiento	birth
la Nochebuena	Christmas Eve
la Nochevieja	New Year's Eve
la Pascua	Easter
mandar	to send
postales de Navidad	Christmas cards
encender velas	to light candles
un desfile	a procession
fuegos artificiales	fireworks
dar / recibir	to give / receive
regalos	presents
comemos	we eat

bebimos	we drink
jugamos a juegos	we play games
visito a mis abuelos	I visit my grandparents
damos regalos	we give presents
recibimos regalos	we receive presents
mi regalo favorito fue	my favourite present was
celebramos	we celebrate
vemos la tele	we watch TV
nos divertimos	we have fun
descansamos	we relax
nos reímos	we laugh
vienen a vernos	they come to see us
vamos a verlos	we go to see them
no nos vemos mucho	we don't see each other much
pasamos tiempo juntos	we spend time together
aprovechamos	we make the most of
la oportunidad	the opportunity

Example

En Inglaterra no hay tantas fiestas como en España. Me encantaría ir a una fiesta española como la Tomatina cerca de Valencia, donde la gente se lanza tomates durante unas horas. Es una tradición muy curiosa, pero parece divertida.

In England there aren't as many festivals as in Spain. I'd love to go to a Spanish festival like the Tomatina near Valencia, where people throw tomatoes at each other for a few hours. It is a strange tradition but it seems fun.

EDUCATION AND EMPLOYMENT

School and lessons

un colegio	a school
un insti	a school
mi escuela primaria	my primary school
un internado	boarding school
una escuela de niñas	a girls' school
una escuela de niños	a boys' school

School positives

el mejor colegio	the best school
del mundo	in the world
lo que más me gusta	what I like most
los profes son buenos	the teachers are good
los alumnos	the pupils
mucho que hacer	lots to do
tengo muchos amigos	I have lots of friends

School negatives

lo que no me gusta	what I don't like
tenemos que	we have to
llevar un uniforme	wear a uniform
los profes nos dan	the teachers give us
demasiados deberes	too much homework
las reglas son estrictas	the rules are strict
no se puede	you can't
comer chicle	to chew gum
usar el móvil	to use a mobile

llevar joyas	to wear jewellery
llevar maquillaje	to wear make-up

Facilities

aulas	classrooms *(teacher = wise owl)*
laboratorios	laboratories
una biblioteca	a library
un comedor	a dining room
campos deportivos	sports fields
una piscina	a pool
el patio	the playground
donde se puede	where you can
paso tiempo leyendo	I spend time reading
jugar	to play
charlar	to chat
estudiar	to study

Example

Hay un campo deportivo donde se puede jugar al futbol, un patio donde paso el recreo charlando y una biblioteca donde paso mucho tiempo estudiando.

There's a sports ground where you can play football, a playground where I spend breaktime chatting and a library where I spend a lot of time studying.

Subjects

las matemáticas	maths
las ciencias / ciencias	sciences
la biología	biology

la química	chemistry
la física	physics
la música	music
la geografía	geography
la historia	history
el francés	French
el inglés	English
el latín	Latin

Example

Me gusta mi colegio porque hay mucho que hacer y los profes son buenos. Mi asignatura favorita es el inglés porque es fácil y el profe es simpático, pero no me gustan las matemáticas porque el profe nos da demasiados deberes.

I like my school because there is a lot to do and the teachers are good. My favourite subject is English because it's easy and the teacher is nice but I don't like maths because the teacher gives us too much homework.

Education verbs

enseñar	to teach *(you need to be 'senior')*
aprender	to learn *(an apprentice learns)*
sacar buenas notas	to get good marks *(out of the sack)*
tener éxito	to succeed *(exciting!)*
revisar	to revise
pasar exámenes	to take exams
aprobar un examen	to pass an exam *(probably?)*
sacarse un reprobado	to fail *(reprobate!)*
preguntar	to ask
contestar	to answer *(in a contest)*

poner pruebas	to give tests

School day

al llegar	on arriving
a las ocho	at 8 o'clock
las clases empiezan	lessons begin
cada clase dura	each lesson lasts
ocho clases al día	eight lessons a day
la hora de comer	the lunch hour
el descanso	break time
el recreo	break time
las clases terminan	lessons finish
vuelvo a casa	I go home

Plans for the future

seguir estudiando	to carry on studying
para que pueda	so that I can
conseguir un buen trabajo	get a good job
cuando sea mayor	when I'm older
ayudar a la gente	to help people
ganar mucho dinero	to earn a lot
viajar por todas partes	travel everywhere
cambiar el mundo	change the world
sobre todo	especially

Example

Voy a seguir trabajando duro para que pueda conseguir un buen empleo. No sé exactamente lo que voy a hacer en el futuro. Lo importante es que sea interesante. Me gustaría sobre todo ayudar a la gente y ganar mucho dinero, pero el dinero tiene menos importancia.

I am going to carry on working hard so I can get a good job. I don't know exactly what I'm going to do in the future. The important thing is that it is interesting. Most of all I'd like to help people and earn lots of money, but the money is less important.

Jobs

un empleo / un trabajo	job
azafata	air hostess
contable	accountant
abogado / -a	lawyer
hombre / mujer de negocios	businessman / businesswoman
profesor /-a	teacher
científico /-a	scientist
peluquero /-a	hairdresser
periodista	journalist
enfermero /-a	nurse
marinero /-a	sailor
escultor /-a	sculptor
escritor /-a	writer
pescador /-a	fisherman
bombero /-a	fireman
panadero /-a	baker
matador	bullfighter
ingeniero /-a	engineer
cantante	singer

Part time jobs

a tiempo parcial	part-time
experiencia laboral	work experience
ganar un sueldo	to earn a salary
trabajaba	I used to work
ganaba	I used to earn
tenía que	I had to
poner las mesas	lay the tables
preparar las verduras	prepare the vegetables
limpiar la cocina	clean the kitchen
servir a los clientes	serve the clients
recibía propinas	I used to get tips
ahorré mi dinero	I saved my money
un aprendizaje	apprenticeship
una compañía	a company
una empresa	a business

SOCIAL ACTIVITIES AND HEALTH

Healthy lifestyle

la salud	health
malo para la salud	bad for your health
bueno para la salud	good for your health
sano / saludable	healthy
unos consejos	some advice
llevar una vida sana	to lead a healthy life
una dieta sana	a healthy diet
una dieta equilibrada	a balanced diet
la cantidad	quantity *(dad= ity)*
cinco porciones de	5 portions of
fruta y verduras	fruit and vegetables
deberíamos	we should
intentar	to try to
comer sano	eat healthily
evitar	avoid
la comida basura	junk food
el azúcar	sugar
la materia grasa	fat *(greasy)*
alimentos sanos	healthy food
el alcohol	alcohol
tomar drogas	to take drugs
fumar porros	to smoke joings
hacer ejercicio	to do exercise
hacer deporte	to do sport
al aire libre	in the fresh air
dormir	to sleep

puede causar	it can cause
enfermedades graves	serious illnesses
el cáncer	cancer
la obesidad	obesity
sobrepeso	overweight
perder peso	to lose weight
problemas de oido	hearing problems
se puede	you can
enfermarse	to get sick
engordar	to get fat
aunque sea malo	although it's bad
para la salud	for your health

Leisure

el ocio	leisure
en mi tiempo libre	in my free time
hago deporte	I do sport
juego al tenis	I play tennis
me gusta hacer	I like doing
me gusta jugar	I like playing

Sports that take hacer

deporte	sport
natación	swimming
equitación	horseriding
windsurf	windsurfing
monopatín	skateboarding
vela	sailing *(turn the v over - sail)*

patinaje	skating *(pat the ice)*
gimnástico	gymnastics
ciclismo	cycling
piragüismo	canoeing
tiro con arco	archery
alpinismo	mountaineering
atletismo	athletics
senderismo	hiking

Playing games

jugar al ajedrez	to play chess
jugar a las cartas	to play cards
jugar al baloncesto	to play basketball
jugar al fútbol	to play football
jugar al hockey	to play hockey
jugar al cricket	to play cricket
un partido de fútbol	a football match
asistir a	to attend

People in sport

el jugador	player
el / la futbolista	footballer
el / la tenista	tennis player
el / la ciclista	cyclist
el / la atleta	athlete
el / la torero /-a / matador	bullfighter
el / la campeón /-a	champion
los espectadores	spectators

Sports events

entrenarse	to train
recibir premios	to win prizes
el partido	match
el torneo	tournament
el concurso	competition
la copa del mundo	the world cup
el campeonato	championship
la carrera	race
en equipo	in a team
el equipo escolar	the school team

Other hobbies

leer periódicos	read newspapers
leer libros	books
leer revistas	read magazines *(reveiws)*
novelas	novels
tebeos	comics
la lectura	reading
dibujar	to draw
pintar	to paint
dar paseos	to go for walks
ir de compras	to go shopping
escuchar música	to listen to music
ver la tele	to watch TV
tocar el piano	to play piano *(toc toc toc)*
tocar la guitarra	to play guitar
cantar	to sing *(chant)*

bailar	to dance *(ballet)*
coleccionar	to collect
pescar	to fish
chatear en línea	to chat online
compartir fotos	to share photos
descansar	to relax

Example

En mi tiempo libre, me gusta pasar horas chateando en línea, en las redes sociales, enviando mensajes y compartiendo fotos. También juego al tenis y veo la tele.

In my free time I like to spend hours online chatting on social networks, sending messages and sharing photos. I also play tennis and watch TV.

Cinema and TV

ir al cine	to go to the cinema
ver la tele	to watch TV
una película	a film *(about pelicans?)*
mi película favorita	my favourite film
mi programa favorito	my favourite programme
el canal	channel
telenovelas	soaps
telebasura	rubbish TV
documentales	documentaries
las noticias	the news *(notices)*
educativa	educational
una herramienta útil	a useful tool *(hairy-men tools)*
acabo de ver	I have just seen

una película de horror	horror film
una película de ciencia ficción	sci fi film
una película de guerra	war film
una película policiaca	detective film
una película del oeste	western
una película de amor	romantic film
una película de aventuras	adventure film
dibujos animados	cartoons
trata de	it's about
efectos especiales	special effects

Illness

hay el riesgo de	there is the risk of
una enfermedad	an illness
enfermo /-a	ill
estar mal	to be unwell
sentirse	to feel
me siento	I feel
toser	to cough
la tos	cough
vomitar	to vomit
estar constipado	to have a cold
un resfriado	a cold
el sida	AIDS
el dolor	pain
una picadura	a bite / sting
la gripe	flu
ir al médico	to go to the doctor

pastillas	pills
medicina	medicine
medicamentos	medicine
sufrir	to suffer

Accidents

un accidente	an accident
tuve un accidente	I had an accident
tuvo un accidente	he / she had an accident
me rompí la pierna	I broke my leg
el incendio	a fire
apagar el incendio	to put out a fire
el humo	the smoke
la inundación	the flood
el peligro	the danger
un pinchazo	a puncture
tuve un pinchazo	I had a puncture
el riesgo	the risk
sangre	blood
una multa	a fine
ayudar	to help
salvar	to save
gritar	to shout
chocar / pegar / golpear	to hit
atropellar	to run over
ocurrir / suceder	to happen
ahogarse	to drown
el herido	the injured person
en la cárcel	in prison

Body parts

el brazo	arm
la mano	hand *(the main thing you need)*
el dedo	finger
el pie	foot
la pierna	leg *(longer than el pie)*
la rodilla	knee
la espalda	back
la cara	face
la oreja / el oído	ear
la cabeza	head *(cabbage)*
la nariz	nose
el estómago	stomach
el pelo	hair
el diente / la muela	tooth
la voz	voice
los ojos	eyes
los hombros	shoulders *(hombres - men)*
la boca	mouth *(bocadillo = sandwich)*

FOOD AND DRINK

Eating meals

comer	to eat
desayunar	to have breakfast
desayuno tostadas	I have toast for breakfast
almorzar	to have lunch
el almuerzo	lunch
cenar	to have dinner
la cena	dinner
la merienda	tea
pedir	to ask for
probar	to try
la cocina	cooking / the kitchen
cocinar	to cook

General food

pan	bread
tostadas	toast
cereales	cereal
mantequilla	butter *(meant-to-kill-ya)*
mermelada	jam
bocadillos	sandwiches
el arroz	rice
el queso	cheese
postre	pudding
dulces	sweet things
alimentos	food
comida	food

la carne	meat
el pollo	chicken
un bistec	a steak
la carne de vaca	beef (*meat of cow*)
el cerdo	pig / pork
el cordero	lamb
una chuleta	a chop
el jamón	ham
la ternera	veal
una hamburguesa	a hamburger
pescado	fish

las verduras	vegetables
las judías verdes	green beans
el pimiento	pepper
los guisantes	peas
la ensalada	salad
los champiñones	mushrooms (*champions*)
la lechuga	lettuce
el tomate	tomato
las zanahorias	carrots (bigger *than-your-ears*)
las espinacas	spinach
el espárrago	asparagus
la coliflor	cauliflower
las patatas	potatoes
las patatas fritas	chips
el pepino	cucumber
las cebollas	onions (*they-boil-ya*)

las frutas — fruit

las frutas	fruit
la naranja	orange
las uvas	grapes
la cereza	cherry
el limón	lemon
las manzanas	apples *(man has Adam's apple)*
el plátano	banana *(curls around a plate)*
el melocotón	peach *(peach skin feels cottony)*
la pera	pear
la pina	pineapple
el albaricoque	apricot
el helado	ice cream
caramelos	sweets
pasteles	cakes

Las bebidas — drinks

Las bebidas	drinks
una cerveza	beer
la leche	milk
un té	tea
un café	coffee
un vino tinto	red wine
un vino blanco	white wine
el agua	water
zumo	juice
una limonada	lemonade
cubitos	ice cubes
el hielo	ice
refrescos	soft drinks

en el restaurante	in the restaurant
los platos	plates
el tenedor	fork
la cuchara	spoon
el cuchillo	knife
el vaso	a glass
el camarero	waiter
la cuenta	the bill
la propina	the tip

MODERN WORLD AND ENVIRONMENT

el medioambiente	environment
los coches emiten	cars emit
gases tóxicos	toxic gases
las fábricas	factories
los gases suben	the gases rise up
en la atmosfera	into the atmosphere
causan	they cause
la contaminación del aire	air pollution
el calentamiento global	global warming
el efecto invernadero	the greenhouse effect
los mares suben	the sea levels are rising
en peligro	in danger
el problema	the problem
va empeorando	is getting worse
amenazar	to threaten *(menace)*
los vertidos nucleares	nuclear waste
deberíamos	we should

se debe / hay que	it is necessary to
salvar	to save
proteger	to protect
mejorar	to improve
actuar	to act
los recursos naturales	natural resources
agotarse	to run out
el derretimiento de las capas de hielo	melting of ice-caps

Example

Lo que más me preocupa es la contaminación del aire en las ciudades. Deberíamos usar el transporte público y abandonar los coches. Además, si hubiera más rutas para ciclistas podríamos ir en bici en vez de en coche. Cuando sea mayor, voy a seguir protegiendo el medioambiente para que los recursos naturales no se agoten.

What worries me most is air pollution in the cities. We should use public transport and leave our cars behind. Also, if there were more cycle paths we could go by bike instead of by car. When I'm older I'm going to carry on protecting the environment so that natural resources don't run out.

What do you for the environment?

ducharse – me ducho	to shower
para ahorrar agua	to save water
apagar las luces - apago	to turn off the lights
para ahorrar electricidad	to save electricity
reciclar - reciclo	to recycle
el cartón	cardboard
el vidrio y el plástico	glass and plastic

el contenedor	container
los envases	packaging
usar - uso	to use
el transporte público	public transport
ir en bici / hacer ciclismo	to cycle
comprar productos ecológicos	buy green products

Social problems

los sintecho	the homeless *(without a roof)*
dormir al raso	to sleep rough
duermen	they sleep *(radical changing)*
la pobreza	poverty
el mendigo	beggar *(clothes need mending)*
la inmigración	immigration
los inmigrantes	immigrants
los refugiados	refugees
un refugio	refuge
la falta de dinero	lack of money *(it's a fault)*
la falta de casas	lack of houses
sin familias	without families
familias monoparentales	single parent families
el paro	unemployment
las drogas	drugs
drogas blandas	soft drugs
piensan que es guay	they think it's cool
a largo plazo	in the long term
las cifras dan miedo	the figures are alarming
recaudar fondos	to raise funds

de segunda mano	second hand
trabajo voluntario	volunteering

La publicidad

	publicity
los anuncios	adverts
las medias	the media
la responsabilidad	responsibility
animar a…. a…	to encourage …. to…
quieren ser	they want to be
más delgado	thinner
más popular	more popular
más guay	cooler
influidos por	influenced by
por todas partes	everywhere
una mala influencia	a bad influence
por muchas razones	for many reasons
nocivo	harmful
informativo	informative
poderoso	powerful
lanzar una campaña	to launch a campaign
piensan que necesitan	they think they need
crear la avidez	create greed

Technology

la tecnología	technology
soy adicto	I'm addicted
no puedo prescindir de	I can't do without
el móvil	the mobile phone

el ordenador	the computer
enviar mensajes	to send messages
ponerse al día	to get up to date
navegar el internet	to surf the internet
descargar	to download
colgar	to post
bloquear	to block
guardar	to sabe
borrar	to delete
grabar	to record
el buzón	inbox
películas y música	films and music
las redes sociales	social networks
una página web	a website
ponerse en contacto con	to get in touch with
buscar información	to look up information

Technology dangers

Hablar con desconocidos	talk to strangers
problemas de vista	eyesight problems
pegado a la pantalla	glued to the screen
perder amigos	to lose friends
volverse solitario	to get lonely
volverse triste	to get depressed
causar accidentes	to cause accidents
cruzas la calle mirándolo	you cross the road looking at it
se vuelven	they become
adicto(s)	addicted

obeso	obese
hay el riesgo de	there is the risk of
el robo de identidad	identity theft
ciber intimidación	cyber-bullying
la piratería	hacking

Example

No puedo prescindir de mi móvil. Acabo de recibirlo para mi cumpleaños y lo uso para todo, para enviar mensajes, para descargar música y películas y para buscar información. Lo malo es que hay muchos peligros también. Se puede hablar con desconocidos en las redes sociales sin saber quiénes son. Uno puede volverse solitario y perder amigos, pasando todo el día pegado a la pantalla.

I can't do without my mobile. I just received it for my birthday and I use it for everything – to send messages, to download music and films and to look up information. The bad thing is that there are lots of dangers as well. You can talk to strangers on social networks without knowing who they are. One can get lonely and lose friends by spending all day glued to the screen.

General vocabulary lists

Time

son las dos y media	it's 2.30
son las ocho y cuarto	it's 8.15
son las tres menos cuarto	it's 2.45
es la una menos diez	it's 12.50
a las dos	at 2 o'clock
a la una	at 1 o'clock
a mediodía	at midday
a medianoche	at midnight

Adverbial time phrases and adverbs of time

hoy	today
ayer	yesterday
mañana	tomorrow
la semana pasada	last week
la semana que viene	next week
la semana próxima	next week
el año pasado	last year
el año que viene	next year
el año próximo	next year
el fin de semana pasado	last weekend
el fin de semana que viene	next weekend
el fin de semana próximo	next weekend
hace cinco años	5 years ago
en el pasado	in the past
en el futuro	in the future
cuando sea mayor	when I'm older

Frequency

a veces	sometimes
a menudo	often
de vez en cuando	from time to time
siempre	always
todo el tiempo	all the time
todo el día	all day
nunca	never
normalmente	normally
durante la semana	in the week
los fines de semana	at the weekend
tres veces a la semana	three times a week
todos los días	every day
cada día	each day
por la mañana	in the morning
por la tarde	in the afternoon
por la noche	at night
por lo general	in general

Days

lunes	Monday
martes	Tuesday
miércoles	Wednesday
jueves	Thursday
viernes	Friday
sábado	Saturday
domingo	Sunday

Months

enero	January
febrero	February
marzo	March
abril	April
mayo	May
junio	June
julio	July
agosto	August
septiembre	September
octubre	October
noviembre	November
diciembre	December

Mi cumpleaños es el nueve de mayo. My birthday is 9 May.

Seasons

invierno	Winter
primavera	Spring
verano	Summer
otoño	Autumn

Prepositions

delante de	in front of
detrás de	behind
encima de	above
en	on or in
debajo de	below

cerca de	near
al lado de	next to
lejos de	far from
a unos minutos de	a few minutes from
con	with
sin	without
contra	against
hacia	towards
según	according to
entre	between
hasta	until
a	to, at
de	of, from
fuera de	outside (of)
dentro	inside
en vez de	instead of
en lugar de	instead of

Common -ar verbs

Hablar	to speak
Ayudar	to help
Charlar	to chat
Escuchar	to listen to
Esperar	to wait for or hope
Mirar	to look at
Reciclar	to recycle
Buscar	to look for
Usar	to use

Caminar	to walk
Andar	to walk
Descargar	to download
Llegar	to arrive
Llevar	to wear
Disfrutar	to enjoy
Odiar	to hate
Animar a	to encourage
Encontrar	to find
Olvidar	to forget
Bailar	to dance
Cantar	to sing
Cocinar	to cook
Jugar a	to play
Guardar	to save (IT)
Salvar	to save (planet)
Ahorrar	to save (economise)
Borrar	to delete
Grabar	to record
Pensar	to think
Dar	to give
Crear	to create
Dibujar	to draw
Pintar	to paint
Diseñar	to design
Comprar	to buy
Celebrar	to celebrate
Sacar	to take out

Sacar buenas notas	to get good marks
Sacar fotos	to take photos
Tomar	to take
Fumar	to smoke
Probar	to try
Aumentar	to increase
Bajar	to lower, go down
Bajar del taxi	to get out of the taxi
Opinar	to think
Comentar	to comment on
Fomentar	to develop
Desarrollar	to develop
Trabajar	to work
Ganar	to earn or win
Gastar	to spend
Malgastar	to waste
Preparer	to prepare
Limpiar	to clean
Lavar	to wash
Apagar	to switch off
Pasar la aspiradora	to hoover
Pasar tiempo	to spend time
Ordenar	to tidy
Llamar	to call
Cambiar	to change
Estudiar	to study
Visitar	to visit
Enseñar	to teach

Valorar	to value
Apreciar	to appreciate
Descansar	to relax
Aprovechar	to make the most of
Estar	to be (position, emotion)
Contestar	to answer
Echar de menos	to miss (a person or place)
Pagar	to pay
Necesitar	to need
Faltar	to be missing
Viajar	to travel
Comunicar	to communicate
Engordar	to get fat
Contaminar	to pollute
Informar	to inform
Participar en	to take part in
Provocar	to cause
Causar	to cause
Golpear	to hit
Gritar	to shout
Tratar	to treat
Maltratar	to mistreat

Common -er verbs

Ser	to be
Perder	to lose or miss
Tener	to have
Hacer	to do

Volver	to return
Comer	to eat
Beber	to drink
Poner	to put
Aprender	to learn
Poder	to be able to
Creer	to believe
Deber	to have to
Temer	to be afraid
Mantener	to maintain
Leer	to read
Entender	to hear or understand
Comprender	to understand
Encender	to light or switch on
Ver	to watch
Correr	to run
Esconder	to hide
Responder	to answer
Vender	to sell
Saber	to know (facts)
Conocer	to know (places, people etc)
Promover	to promote

Common -ir verbs

Ir	to go
Abrir	to open
Asistir a	to attend
Subir	to go up – rise

Subir al taxi	to get into a taxi
Recibir	to receive
Decir	to say
Discutir	to argue
Escribir	to write
Construir	to build
Abolir	to abolish
Añadir	to add
Confundir	to confuse
Decidir	to decide
Definir	to define
Cubrir	to cover
Descubrir	to discover
Interrumpir	to interrupt
Prohibir	to prohibit
Unir	to unite
Aplaudir	to applaud
Emitir	to emit
Producir	to produce
Reducir	to reduce
Seguir	to follow or continue

Question words

¿Dónde está…?	Where is…?
¿Adónde vas?	Where are you going?
¿De dónde eres?	Where are you from?
¿Quien?	Who
¿Cuándo?	When?

¿A qué hora?	At what time?
¿Cuál es...?	What / which is...?
¿Qué es...?	What is...?
¿Por qué?	Why...?
¿Cómo...?	How...?
¿Cuántos...?	How many...?

Countries

Austria	Austria
Belgium	Bélgica
Denmark	Dinamarca
England	Inglaterra
France	Francia
Germany	Alemania
Great Britain	Gran Bretaña
Greece	Grecia
Holland	Holanda
Ireland	Irlanda
Italy	Italia
Netherlands	Países bajos (m pl)
Russia	Rusia
Scotland	Escocia
Spain	España
Sweden	Suecia
Switzerland	Suiza
United Kingdom	Reino Unido
United States	Estados Unidos
Wales	País de Gales

Continents

Africa	África
Asia	Asia
Australia	Australia
Europe	Europa
North America	América del Norte
South America	América del Sur

Nationalities

American	americano/a
Austrian	austriaco /a
Belgian	belga
British	británico/a
Dutch	holandés/a
English	inglés/a
European	europeo/a
French	francés/a
German	alemán/a
Greek	griego/a
Irish	irlandés/a
Italian	italiano/a
Russian	ruso/a
Scottish	escocés/a
Spanish	español/a
Swedish	sueco/a
Swiss	suizo/a
Welsh	galés/a

Other publications also available on Amazon:

How to Ace your French oral

How to Ace your Spanish oral

How to Ace your German oral

French vocabulary for GCSE

Spanish vocabulary for GCSE

The Common Entrance French Handbook

Brush up your French – a revision guide for grown-ups

The A level French handbook

The French GCSE handbook

Ten Magic tricks with French

Spanish in a week

Advanced French Conversation

Advanced French Vocabulary

Countdown to French GCSE

Countdown to Spanish GCSE

If you have any comments or questions on any of the content of this book, please do get in touch via my website

www.lucymartintuition.co.uk

Find me on Facebook and like my page to be first in the running for news and offers and free books!

And for some extra tips on how to impress examiners with your oral and writing, subscribe to my Lucy Martin Tuition YouTube channel.

Printed in Great Britain
by Amazon